Sherry Kinkoph Gunter

Sams **Teach Yourself**

Facebook®

in **10 Minutes**

SAMS | 800 East 96th Street, Indianapolis, Indiana 46240

Sams Teach Yourself Facebook® in 10 Minutes

ISBN-13: 978-0-672-33087-2
ISBN-10: 0-672-33087-3

Library of Congress Cataloging-in-Publication data is on file.

Printed in the United States of America

First Printing August 2009

Trademarks

Warning and Disclaimer

Bulk Sales

Pearson Education, Inc. offers excellent discounts on this book when ordered in quantity for bulk purchases or special sales. For more information, please contact

U.S. Corporate and Government Sales

1-800-382-3419

corpsales@pearsontechgroup.com

For sales outside of the U.S., please contact

International Sales

international@pearson.com

Associate Publisher
Greg Wiegand

Acquisitions Editor
Michelle Newcomb

Development Editor
Joyce Nielsen

Managing Editor
Patrick Kanouse

Project Editor
Jennifer Gallant

Copy Editor
Water Crest Publishing, Inc.

Indexer
Tim Wright

Technical Editor
Vince Averello

Publishing Coordinator
Cindy Teeters

Book Designer
Anne Jones

Compositor
Bronkella Publishing LLC

Contents

About the Author

Sherry Kinkoph Gunter has written and edited oodles of books over the past 17 years covering a wide variety of computer topics, including Microsoft Office programs, digital photography, and Web applications. Her recent titles include *Craigslist for Everyone*, *Teach Yourself VISUALLY Microsoft Office 2007*, *Microsoft Office 2008 for Mac Bible*, and *Master VISUALLY Dreamweaver and Flash CS3*. Sherry began writing computer books back in '92 for Macmillan, and her flexible writing style has allowed her to author for a varied assortment of imprints and formats. Sherry's ongoing quest is to aid users of all levels in the mastering of ever-changing computer technologies, helping users make sense of it all and get the most out of their machines and online experiences. Sherry currently resides in a swamp in the wilds of east central Indiana with a lovable ogre and a menagerie of interesting creatures. Sherry is also hopelessly addicted to Facebook.

Dedication

Special thanks go out to Michelle Newcomb for allowing me the opportunity to tackle this exciting project; to development editor Joyce Nielsen, for her dedication and patience in shepherding this project; to copy editor Sarah Kearns, for ensuring that all the i's were dotted and t's were crossed; to technical editor Vince Averello, for skillfully checking each step and offering valuable input along the way; and finally to the production team at Pearson, for their talents in creating such a helpful, much-needed, and incredibly good-looking book. Also, special thanks to my loveable cohort, Matty, for his constant support and irrepressible humor. Lastly, extra-special thanks to all my Facebook friends and their avid interest in helping with this project.

We Want to Hear from You!

As the reader of this book, *you* are our most important critic and commentator. We value your opinion and want to know what we're doing right, what we could do better, what areas you'd like to see us publish in, and any other words of wisdom you're willing to pass our way.

You can email or write me directly to let me know what you did or didn't like about this book—as well as what we can do to make our books stronger.

Please note that I cannot help you with technical problems related to the topic of this book, and that due to the high volume of mail I receive, I might not be able to reply to every message.

When you write, please be sure to include this book's title and author as well as your name and phone or email address. I will carefully review your comments and share them with the author and editors who worked on the book.

E-mail: consumer@samspublishing.com

Mail: Greg Wiegand
        Associate Publisher
        Sams Publishing
        800 East 96th Street
        Indianapolis, IN 46240 USA

Reader Services

Visit our website and register this book at informit.com/register for convenient access to any updates, downloads, or errata that might be available for this book.

Introduction

Anyone in the know has heard the buzz about Facebook. It's a hot topic these days, and shows no signs of letting up. If you're ready to get to the bottom of this Internet sensation and find out how to utilize this social networking phenomenon for yourself, this is the book for you. Social networks are a bit daunting at first, but don't worry. This book will show you how to navigate the site and make use of its various features in no time at all. By the end, you'll feel like you can Facebook with the best of them!

About This Book

As part of the *Sams Teach Yourself in 10 Minutes* guides, this book aims to teach you the ins and outs of using Facebook without wasting a lot of precious time. Divided into easy-to-handle lessons that you can tackle in 10 minutes each, you learn the following Facebook tasks and topics:

- ▶ How to painlessly set up a Facebook account
- ▶ How to create and manage a profile page, including how to add a profile picture
- ▶ How to connect with friends and make new ones
- ▶ How to communicate by messaging, chatting, and posting status updates
- ▶ How to track what your friends are doing and what they're up to on Facebook
- ▶ How to upload photos and videos to share with friends
- ▶ How to share your common interests and hobbies through groups
- ▶ How to add applications to get more out of your Facebook experience
- ▶ How to sell and buy stuff in the Marketplace

- ▶ How to use Facebook's mobile features

- ▶ How to create pages for a professional business or organization

- ▶ How to keep yourself safe on Facebook

- ▶ How to conduct yourself on the site and follow Facebook's terms of service and unspoken etiquette rules

After completing these lessons, you'll know everything you need to know to get the most out of your time on Facebook.

Who This Book Is For

This book is geared toward anyone interested in learning their way around Facebook. Whether you're a new user or a seasoned participant, or you're just learning how to navigate the new and improved interface, this book shows you each major feature of the site and how to make use of it. For example, have you always wanted to start your own group? Have you ever wondered how to invite people to a party? Or perhaps you've always wanted to look for more applications to try but didn't know how to find them? You'll learn how to do these tasks, and more.

Each lesson focuses on a particular subject, such as communicating on Facebook or using the Photos application. You can skip around from topic to topic, or read the book from start to finish.

What Do I Need to Use This Book?

To use this book, all you really need is a healthy dose of curiosity to find out what you can do on Facebook. To use Facebook itself, you'll need a computer, a web browser, and an Internet connection. That's it. Facebook is free to use, so if you've got those three things, you're all set.

Conventions Used in This Book

Whenever you need to click a particular button or link in Facebook, you'll find the label or name for that item bolded in the text, such as "click the **Delete** button." In addition to the text and figures in this book, you'll also encounter some special boxes labeled Tip, Note, or Caution.

> **Tip**
> Tips offer helpful shortcuts or easier ways to do something.

> **Note**
> Notes are extra bits of information related to the text that might help you expand your knowledge or understanding.

> **Caution**
> Cautions are warnings or other important information you need to know about consequences of using a feature or executing a task.

Screen Captures

The figures captured for this book are mainly from the Internet Explorer web browser (version 8.0). If you use a different browser, your screens may look slightly different.

Also keep in mind that the developers of Facebook are constantly working to improve the website. New features are added regularly, and old ones change or disappear. This means the pages change often, including the elements found on each, so your own screens may differ from the ones shown in this book. Don't be too alarmed, however. The basics, though they are tweaked in appearance from time to time, stay mostly the same in principle and usage.

Introduction to Facebook

In this lesson, you learn about the Facebook phenomenon, where it came from, and what you can do with it.

What Is Facebook?

Facebook is a social networking website. To flesh out this definition a bit more, it's an online community—a place where people can meet and interact; swap photos, videos, and other information; and generally connect with friends, family, coworkers, fellow students, fellow hobbyists and enthusiasts, and numerous others in their social network. Facebook connects people within cities or regions, work or school, home or abroad, and so on. Built on an architecture of profile pages that allow individual users to share information about themselves and communicate with others, Facebook seeks to create an environment in which members log in regularly to keep track of what friends and colleagues are doing, share their own activities, interact about interests and hobbies, send messages, and join groups and networks—just to name a few things.

Facebook is fast becoming the most popular social networking site on the Internet, quickly surpassing the previous leader, MySpace, in the number of registered users. Offering free access and dozens of tools for connecting people in social, school, and workplace environments, Facebook has over 200 million active users and is growing, with 100 million logging in daily to use the site. Over 30 million users access Facebook through mobile devices. Perhaps you're wondering at this point why so many people are flocking to Facebook? That's easy—it's incredibly simple to use.

What started out as a college-based social network site, two-thirds of Facebook's members are now outside of the college startup base and include users of all ages and walks of life. In other words, Facebook isn't just for college kids anymore. One of the fastest-growing segments of users is the 35–54-year-old crowd.

Facebook is also a global phenomenon. Over 40 translations of the site are up and running, with more in development. 70% of users are outside the U.S., but those numbers are changing as Facebook rapidly catches on in the states.

At its heart, Facebook is all about connecting people with people. Facebook users do a variety of things with the site: track news about friends far and wide; make new friends centered around common interests; share photos, music, links, and videos; organize and invite people to events; play games; spread the word about charities and causes; buy and sell stuff; market products; and much, much more.

As a website, Facebook is accessible to all Internet users, where permitted. In addition to connecting people, third-party developers are creating a wide variety of applications—programs that run within the Facebook framework—to entertain and inform. Applications range from the silly to the serious, and new ones are added each day. What makes Facebook such a huge hit is its features and tools, and the willingness of its users to network with each other in their communities locally and globally.

Facebook History

Social networks have been around for awhile now, and most are focused on connecting friends and colleagues. Bulletin Board Services (BBS) and Usenet groups were examples of early forms of social networks. As the concept evolved, generalized communities, like Geocities and Tripod (back in the mid-1990s), brought people together through chat rooms and forums. Today, social networks are flourishing all over the Web, including the ever-popular MySpace, Twitter, and LinkedIn. Some social sites, like Classmates.com, specialize in connecting former schoolmates, whereas other social sites, such as SixDegrees.com, focus on indirect ties between people. Some sites specialize in niche groups, whereas others aim for more generalized populations of people. Internet business strategies are recognizing the opportunities inherent in social networks and are happy to cater to different groups of people and their networking needs.

So where does Facebook fit in? Facebook is quickly becoming a front runner in the social networking race. Originally called *The Facebook*, Facebook started out in 2004 as a network geared toward college students at Harvard University. Founded by a computer science major, Mark Zuckerberg, and his roommates, Dustin Moskovitz and Chris Hughes, the project quickly gained popularity among students. With financing assistance from Eduardo Saverin, the site grew seemingly overnight.

The original idea was based on paper *face books* commonly used to acquaint students with the campus community, including staff, faculty, and incoming students. Initially, the website was only available to Harvard students, but rapidly expanded to other universities in the Boston, Massachusetts area. Eventually, the concept spread to other universities and high schools, and today, anyone with a valid email address can join the fray. Facebook swiftly became an Internet sensation, and in 2005, the facebook.com domain was purchased and the base of operations moved to California.

Although the site is free to join, it generates revenue through advertising, including banner ads. New features and updates are added regularly, and the Facebook folks are quick to heed the ideas, wants, and needs of its members. In 2007, the Facebook Platform was launched, allowing a framework for software developers to create applications for the site. Today, tens of thousands of applications are available for Facebook, with more added daily.

Facebook Uses

So what does a Facebook member do on the site? What exactly does the site have to offer? More importantly, what can I get out of the experience? Here's a list of various activities and pursuits to get you started on the road to answers to those questions:

- ▶ Connect with people. Connect with friends, family, colleagues, and fellow students. Reconnect with old friends, acquaintances, and family members scattered about the globe. Make new friends who share your interests.

▶ Keep track of your friends' activities, while they keep track of yours.

▶ Share messages, links, photo albums, and video clips.

▶ Blog with the Facebook Notes feature.

▶ Organize events and invite friends to parties, concerts, band performances, meetings, and gatherings of all kinds.

▶ Play games with friends.

▶ Send virtual gifts, birthday greetings, and other digital objects.

▶ Join in groups and networks to connect with people sharing similar interests.

▶ Become a fan of a celebrity, politician, band, television show, or business.

▶ Buy and sell stuff in the Facebook Marketplace.

▶ Share a resume, or find an employer or an employee.

▶ Collaborate on project info at work or school.

▶ Market yourself, your products, or your company.

This list is just the tip of the iceberg. There's plenty more to do and see, and plenty of people to meet. So what are you waiting for? Log on and start socializing!

Looking at Facebook Pages

The Facebook makers have kept the site fairly simple, which is a major part of its appeal. Naysayers complain that there's not enough customizing options, but truthfully, most customizing that takes place on personal web pages these days usually ends up making the pages distracting and difficult to follow. Navigationally, Facebook includes a logon page as the

starting point for entering the website. After you pass that, you're presented with a Home page, shown in Figure 1.1, and links to your other pages.
Your other pages include your profile page, a Friends page, and your
Inbox. You can easily move between pages by clicking the links at the top
of the Facebook page located in the blue navigation bar. The left side of
the bar has links to your pages, whereas the right side of the bar offers
links to settings, logging out, and a search tool.

FIGURE 1.1 Here's an example of a Home page on Facebook, where a
scrolling news feed appears, along with advertisements and other bits of
information.

If you scroll to the bottom of any Facebook page, you'll find links for
advertisers, developers, terms of service, help, and more. Also at the bottom of the Facebook page is an Applications Bar, which stocks shortcut
links to your favorite Facebook apps.

The Home page (see Figure 1.1) is sort of like Grand Central Station for
news about your friends on Facebook. It tracks the ongoing status updates
of your friends, published photos and videos, shared links, fan pages

they've joined, and so forth. All the activities come together on a scrollable page that's constantly changing (if you refresh the page, that is). The Home page is where you go to see and be seen on Facebook.

As mentioned previously, the focus in Facebook is on profile pages—the place where you add information about yourself to share with others. Figure 1.2 shows an example of a profile page. A typical profile page includes a picture, a status text box so you can let the rest of the Facebook world know what you're up to or what you're thinking, a Wall of activities you're pursuing and communications from friends, and tabs for accessing other pages and features. For example, to add or edit profile information, you can click the **Info** tab to view your details and make changes.

FIGURE 1.2 Here's an example of a profile page on Facebook.

You can view your friend's profile pages to check out what they're doing and what they're up to on Facebook. The information you see listed on your Facebook pages is always changing based on your activities and the activities of your friends, so be sure to refresh your pages often.

So far, I've only described a few of the pages you'll encounter. There are lots more. Now that you've had a brief tour, you're ready to jump in, right? If you haven't created an account yet, Lesson 2, "Setting Up a Profile," shows you how. If you're already a Facebook member, move onto the other lessons detailing how to use the site and get the most out of your social networking experience. Enjoy!

Summary

In this lesson, you learned about social networking sites and how Facebook got its start. You also learned about the various things you can do on the site and what to expect when you start viewing pages. In the next lesson, you learn how to sign up for a Facebook account and start building your profile page.

LESSON 2

Setting Up a Profile

In this lesson, you learn how to sign up for a Facebook account, create a profile, and specify a current status. This information covers everything you need to get started as a Facebook member.

Signing Up for an Account

If you're new to Facebook, the first thing you need to do is sign up for an account. Joining Facebook is free, and the only requirements are that you have a working email address—in other words, a real email address—and you must be thirteen years of age or older. At the end of the registration process, Facebook sends you a confirmation email you must follow to finish setting up your account. The process is relatively painless and fast.

> **Note**
>
> If you want to create a professional account, such as a profile page for a band or business, you can click the link "To create a page for a celebrity, band, or business, **click here**." located on the Facebook Sign Up page (see Figure 2.1). Learn more about the professional and promotional sides of Facebook in Lesson 13, "The Professional Side of Facebook: Pages."

When creating a Facebook account, you need to use your real name. The whole social networking architecture of the site is built on the authenticity of its users. Odd nicknames, pseudonyms, or aliases are simply not allowed. In fact, if you try to use an odd-looking name, it will probably be flagged by Facebook as a possible bogus account. For example, if you attempt to create an account for Lone Ranger, chances are it will not make it. If the name happens to be your real, honest-to-goodness name, you can appeal to Facebook by clicking the **Help** link on the Sign Up page.

To sign up for an account, follow these steps:

1. Use your web browser to display the Facebook Welcome page, **www.facebook.com**.

2. You can start the registration process rolling by filling out the initial sign-up form, shown in Figure 2.1. Click inside the first form box and fill in your full name.

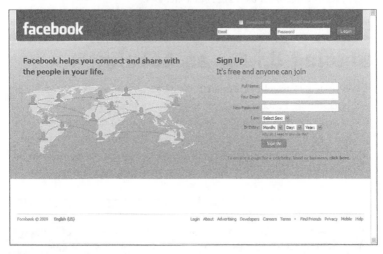

FIGURE 2.1 Facebook's Welcome page is the place to start when you want to create a new account.

3. Type in your email address.

4. Establish a password. As with most passwords you use on the Internet, choose one that contains both numbers and letters for maximum security.

5. Click the **I am** field and select your gender.

6. Click the **Birthday** fields to specify your date of birth. Don't worry—you don't have to show this on your profile page if you don't want to. This information is a security measure to make sure you're old enough to use the site.

7. Click the **Sign Up** button when you're ready to continue.

8. The next phase of the registration process is the security check. Type in the words shown on the screen.

Tip

If you have difficulty reading the wavy words on the Security Check page, you can click the option for changing the words to a new set or listening to an audio file instead.

---

9. Click the **Sign Up** button to continue.

Note

It's a fact that people rarely read the terms of service and privacy policy when signing up for things. In case you were wondering, Facebook's policies basically say you're not allowed to send spam or post pirated material, and you're expected to be honest and nice to everyone online. They also say you cannot hold Facebook accountable if you get into trouble. See Lesson 4, "Finding Help with Facebook Services and Etiquette" to learn more about the terms of service.

Facebook tells you it's going to confirm your address. This may happen quite quickly, and Facebook may continue on to a Getting Started page. If not, proceed to Step 10. If you're already viewing the Getting Started page, you can continue with the sign-up process.

10. Finally, Facebook sends you an email confirmation. When you open the email message, click the link or cut and paste it into your browser to finish up the registration process.

When you click the confirmation link Facebook sends you in an email, Facebook opens in a new browser window to a login page. Login using your new password and confirm your account, if needed, by clicking **Okay**. Depending on your setup, you may now find yourself with two open browser windows showing the same page. You can close one window and keep going.

When you see a page similar to Figure 2.2 in your browser window you're ready to proceed. This next page is the Getting Started section of registering and creating your Facebook account. There are actually three pages you'll jump through as the next phase of your registration. Each page asks you to do something, such as look up friends using your email contacts, specify profile info about your education or job, and join a network. You can choose to pursue each page's options right then and there and add all the necessary details, or you can skip all three and fill in the information at a later time. We'll opt for the latter in this lesson.

FIGURE 2.2   The first Getting Started page allows you to search for existing friends on Facebook using your email contacts list.

In Figure 2.2, Facebook wants to know if you want to look up friends by searching through your contacts list and seeing if any matches already have Facebook accounts. You can learn all about how to find friends in Lesson 3, "Connecting with Friends." For now, just click the **Skip this step** link at the bottom of the page to continue onward.

Figure 2.3 shows the second Getting Started page. This time, Facebook wants to get you started on your profile by adding high school, college or university, or company information. You can take the time to fill this out now, or you can do so later. Skip this by clicking the **Skip this step** link and move on to page 3.

FIGURE 2.3   The second Getting Started page lets you specify your school or work associations.

The last Getting Started page, shown in Figure 2.4, offers to assign you to a network. A network is a community, such as your city or geographical area, your workplace, or your educational setting. Here again, you can fill out all of this now, or take care of it later. Click the **Skip this step** link to keep on going.

After jumping through all the Getting Started hoops, Facebook finally shows you a customized Welcome page featuring your name. You can begin customizing your profile or search for people you know. Click the **View and edit your profile** link to start customizing. The next section shows you how to add nitty-gritty data to your profile page.

FIGURE 2.4   The third Getting Started page lets you specify a network.

By the way, now that you're officially a member, you can log off and on again using your email address and password at the main Facebook page. You'll see boxes (form fields) at the top of the page to enter both these pertinent pieces of information. You can even tell the site to remember you so you don't have to keep typing in the info each time. As for logging out, you can click the **Logout** link at the top of the window to exit the site at any time.

Building Your Profile

After you've registered on Facebook and navigated the Getting Started pages, you can start customizing your personal profile right away. A *profile* is simply a collection of information about you, such as your hobbies and interests, where you go to school or work, favorite music or television shows, favorite quote, and so on. Your Facebook profile is visible to your friends and anyone on your network. After you complete the registration process, Facebook starts you out with a bare bones profile page. It's up to you to add the meat.

In the land of Facebook, *profiles* are for individuals, but *pages* are for bands, celebrities, politicians, businesses, and other groups. We'll focus on your individual profile in this lesson. When you finish the Getting Started pages and click the **View and edit your profile** link on the Welcome page, Facebook takes you to your actual profile page, similar to Figure 2.5.

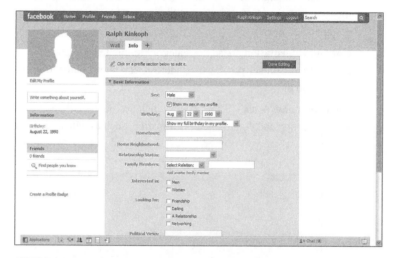

FIGURE 2.5   The bare bones profile page.

You can also navigate to this page at any time during your Facebook session by clicking the **Profile** link in the navigation bar at the top of your Facebook page.

You can change your profile information from the profile page. As you can see in Figure 2.5, the page starts out with several tabs: Wall, Info, and the giant plus sign (which is actually the Add a New Tab tab). There's also an empty profile picture. Any information you added in the sign-up process already appears below the photo area or on the Info tab.

Adding to Your Info

You can start adding more info to your profile by adding to the information shown on your Info tab. You decide what you want to input. You can choose to make a comprehensive profile, or just dole out little bits of information about yourself. As you can see in Figure 2.6, profile info is grouped into several categories:

Basic Information   This group of info includes birthday, gender, hometown, relationship status, and political and religious views.

Personal Information   This category has fields for entering activities and interests, listing favorite things, and whipping up a paragraph about yourself.

Contact Information   Use this category to input information about how to contact you, such as address, cell phone number, website, and so on.

Education and Work   This category includes fields for listing your education and employment information, such as which school you attend, where you work, degrees earned, and so on.

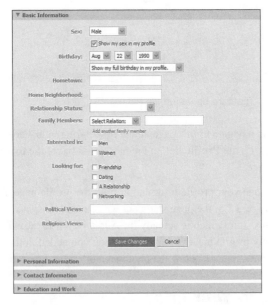

FIGURE 2.6   Profile info is grouped into four categories.

Each category can be expanded or collapsed to view the associated form. Just click a category name, or the gray bar containing the name, to expand or collapse the view. If the categories are not in view at all, you'll need to click the **Edit Information** link in the upper-right corner of the Info tab to switch over to edit view. A pencil icon appears next to the link. Look for the pencil icon anytime you want to make edits to information in Facebook. This particular link toggles the category views on or off, depending on their current status.

To edit any field, click inside the box and start typing. Some fields are text boxes; others are drop-down menus with selections you make. You may notice as you type that Facebook tries to help you with common words and phrases in a pop-up box that appears. You can make selections from the pop-up box and insert them immediately, or you can just ignore the suggestions and keep on typing.

As you make changes to the data in each category, you must click the **Save Changes** button at the bottom of the category to keep your changes. To forgo the edits, click the **Cancel** button instead.

When you save your input, Facebook immediately saves the information and refreshes the page in your browser window.

> **Tip**
>
> If you prefer not to show your full birth date in your profile, click the **Birthday** status drop-down menu located in the Basic Information category group and choose an option, such as **Show only month & day in my profile**. This option is perfect if you want friends to send you birthday greetings on Facebook when your special day arrives.

You'll notice in the Contact Information category that tiny lock icons appear to the far right of some of the form fields. When you click a lock icon, Facebook opens a mini-dialog box that lets you choose who you allow to view the specific contact information. Make your selection and click the **Save** button.

> **Tip**
>
> If you have an account with an instant messaging service, you can add your screen name or alias to your Facebook page using the Contact Information category options. This lets your friends look at your profile and determine if you're logged into your instant message program—a green dot appears next to your screen name when you're logged on.

When you're all finished filling out the profile information, you can click the **Done Editing** button at the top of the page. This turns off the category edit displays and returns you to your profile view.

You can return to edit view at any time and make changes to your info or add new info. You can click the **Edit Information** link on the Info tab of your profile. You can also find a pencil icon in the upper-right corner of any info area box; click this icon to return to the category and make changes to the data.

Adding a Profile Picture

You can add a picture to your profile to help people recognize you or generally add visual interest to your page. Facebook uses your picture as an *avatar*, an image that represents you as you interact with other profiles, groups, and so forth.

If you have a digital image of yourself stored on your computer, you can quickly place it on your page for all to see. If you don't have a portrait photo readily available, you can also insert another type of picture that represents you, such as your favorite hobby or sport. A profile picture can be up to 4MB in file size.

You can choose from several options when adding a picture:

> **Upload a Picture**   This lets you upload a picture you have stored on your computer.
>
> **Take a Picture**   If your computer has a built-in camera, you can use it to take a picture of yourself to place on your Facebook page. Just follow the directions.

Choose from Album Use this option if you want to grab a picture from an existing album you have already placed on Facebook.

Edit Thumbnail This option lets you crop your picture differently, as you see fit.

Remove Your Picture Choose this option to remove the existing profile picture.

Follow these steps to add a picture stored on your computer:

1. Move your mouse pointer over the picture area until you see the **Change Picture** link; click the link.

2. Facebook displays a pop-up menu of options, as shown in Figure 2.7. Click **Upload a Picture**.

FIGURE 2.7 Use this menu to choose how you want to add a picture.

3. The Upload Your Profile Picture dialog box appears, shown in Figure 2.8. Click the **Browse** button.

FIGURE 2.8 The Upload Your Profile Picture dialog box.

4. The Choose File dialog box opens. Navigate to the image file you want to use and double-click the filename (or click it and click **Open**).

   Facebook begins uploading the file. Depending on the file size and your connection speed, the process may take a few moments.

   When the upload is complete, Facebook displays your new picture and adds a new Photos tab to the list of tabs on the page. You may need to refresh the page to view the new Photos tab.

Tip

You can add more than one profile picture to your account and switch between them as the mood strikes you. Facebook stores your profile pictures in the Profile Picture album. You can access the album by clicking the **Photos** tab and then clicking the **Profile Pictures** album. You can then click the **Change Profile Picture** link to swap with another image, upload a new image, or adjust the thumbnail version of the image.

Adding Something About Yourself

Directly below your profile picture is a link for adding something about yourself. You can use this feature to add a note about you, share a quip or motto, pontificate about a subject, or just advertise your latest project. To fill in this info, simply click the **Write something about yourself** link.

An empty text box appears. Type in your information (see Figure 2.9); then click anywhere outside the box. You can always change the info again by clicking the pencil icon in the upper-right corner of the box area.

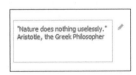

FIGURE 2.9   Type in your info, such as a quote or quip.

Note

You can now create your own personal URL to your Facebook profile page using a unique username. This new feature is handy if you want to direct people directly to your page. To create a Facebook URL, follow this link to set it up: www.facebook.com/username.

Viewing Your Wall

One more thing about your profile page as you're setting things up—you need to check out your Wall. The Wall is a spot where direct social interaction occurs, where you and your friends exchange public messages, and you and others can see your Facebook activities. You can view your Wall by clicking the **Wall** tab on your profile page. New users to Facebook see a Wall similar to Figure 2.10. The Wall is relatively empty at first.

FIGURE 2.10   Behold, the Facebook Wall. It's a mostly empty area when you first start using Facebook.

The Wall is a dynamic, scrollable viewing area, keeping track of your activities and social exchanges. The top of the Wall has a special area for sharing your status, called "What's on your mind?." Below that are some tabs for filtering your view and the scrollable Wall area itself. As you do more with Facebook, more entries are added to the Wall. Others on your Friends list or networks can also view your Wall. You can learn more about using the Wall in Lesson 6, " Tracking Wall Postings, News Feeds, and Notifications." For now, let's focus on changing your status.

Changing Your Status

One way to let others know what you're up to is to post a status update. You can use your status to share a thought, tell people what you're doing at the current moment, or mention other points of interest. Anything you post in the "What's on your mind?" box appears in the newsfeeds of your friends, as well as on your own profile page at the top of your Wall.

In the past, Facebook labeled this status box "What are you doing right now?" and automatically placed the verb "is" in the box for you to add a statement. Users complained about having to deal with the "is" verb, so the Facebook creators changed it. With the latest version of Facebook, the "is" verb is now gone, and you can type whatever you want into the spot.

To change your status, follow these steps:

1. Click in the **What's on your mind?** box and type an entry (see Figure 2.11).

FIGURE 2.11 You can update your status to let people know what you're thinking or what you're doing.

2. Click the **Share** button.

    Facebook adds the status to the top of your profile page (see Figure 2.12), as well as on your Wall. Others can now respond with a comment.

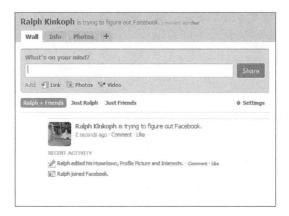

FIGURE 2.12   Facebook adds the new status to your page.

Notice that your status update on the Wall includes your profile picture or avatar. You can also add links, photos, and video clips to your status updates. You'll learn more about using these features in Lesson 6.

Accessing Your Account Info

You can always access your Facebook account info to make changes to your email address, name (if you get married, for example), password, and other settings. To do so, move your mouse pointer over the **Settings** link at the top of the Facebook page; then click **Account Settings** from the drop-down menu. You can also click the **Settings** link directly and then click the **Account Settings** tab.

The My Account page appears, as shown in Figure 2.13. To change any account information in the Settings tab, click the **Change** link next to the area you want to edit and then make the appropriate changes.

To return to your profile page again, click **Profile** at the top of the Facebook page.

Tip

Learn more about changing account settings, such as privacy settings, in Lesson 5, "Guarding Your Privacy." Learn how to control notification settings in Lesson 6.

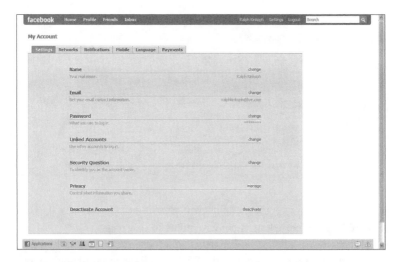

FIGURE 2.13   The Settings tab lets you change basic account details.

Summary

In this lesson, you learned how to sign up for a Facebook account and how to begin building your profile page, including adding information and a photo. You also learned how to update your status and access your account information. In the next lesson, you learn how to start connecting with friends.

Connecting with Friends

In this lesson, you learn how to use the Facebook Friends features to connect with friends online. You learn how to find friends, respond to friend requests, and view and organize friend lists.

Finding Friends

Because you can't really have a social network without friends in some form or fashion, let's get started with learning how to connect with people on Facebook. Many people find themselves invited to join Facebook by their friends who are already online. If this is the case for you, you already have some friend connections to get you started. If you're brand-spanking new to Facebook, you'll have to start finding friends from scratch.

Joining a Network

One of the easiest ways to start connecting on Facebook is to join a network. On Facebook, a network is an online community to which you belong. A network can be as simple as a geographical area, such as your region of the country or your city. Colleges and universities, high schools, companies, and organizations can all be networks on Facebook. When you join a network, anyone else on the network can view your profile (unless you change your profile's privacy setting). By joining a network, your chances of encountering people you know increase dramatically, as well as opportunities for meeting new people who share the same interests.

Depending on the network, such as a school or workplace, you may be required to have a working email address through the organization in order to sign up on their network. If you join a regional or city network, Facebook allows you to join only one area at a time. You cannot be a part of both the Chicago network and the New York City network, for example.

To join a network, follow these steps:

1. Click the **Settings** link on the blue navigation bar; then click **Account Settings**.

2. From the My Account page, click the **Networks** tab. Facebook displays any networks you've joined listed on the left and a field on the right for joining more, as shown in Figure 3.1.

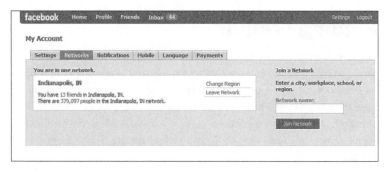

FIGURE 3.1   Use the Networks tab on the My Account page to join networks.

3. Under the Join a Network area, click in the **Network name** box and start typing the workplace, city, region, or school name.

If Facebook recognizes the entry, it displays a list of possible matches. Click one to join. If there are requirements for joining the network, Facebook alerts you.

After you join a network, it's added to the list on the Networks tab. You can use the associated links to change your network region or leave the network entirely if you no longer want to participate.

> **Tip**
> If you don't see a network for your area or company, you can contact Facebook and ask them to create one.

Looking Up Friends

It's easy to look up people on Facebook and establish online connections. For example, if you want to find an old high school chum or look to see if a family member has a profile on the site, you can use the Facebook tools to perform a search. As of this writing, Facebook is revamping its search tools, so the steps and screens you see on your browser window may vary from what you see here. The principles, however, remain the same. You can search for friends to your heart's content using features found on the Friends page, shown in Figure 3.2. Simply click the **Friends** link in the blue navigation bar at the top of the page to navigate to the page. You can also hover your mouse pointer over the **Friends** link in the navigation bar and directly click **Find Friends** to get to the page. The Friends page opens to the Find Friends tools automatically, however, you can always click the Find Friends link to view the tools again later.

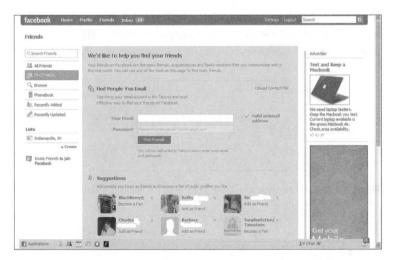

FIGURE 3.2   Use the Friends page to locate friends on Facebook or through your email account.

The Find Friends page is all set up to help you locate friends through your email account, offer friend suggestions if you already have some friends, or search for people by name. The top portion of the page focuses on finding friends based on your email client's address book or contacts list. In other words, Facebook checks your email address book against users' email addresses on the site and tells you about any matches. You'll have to okay access to your email client to perform this task.

> **Note**
>
> To search through your contacts or address book, you must give Facebook the password for the email account. If you're not comfortable doing this, you may want to forgo this search method entirely. To learn more about Facebook's privacy and security settings, see Chapter 5, "Guarding Your Privacy."

The middle portion of the page lists suggestions based on people you've already added to your list. These are typically friends of friends. You can click the **Add as Friend** link beneath a name to invite them to be your friend. This area of the page also lists pages you can become fans of, if interested, that your friends are already supporting.

The bottom portion of the page, shown in Figure 3.3, displays a search tool you can use to look for specific names on Facebook. There's also a tool for looking for connections via your instant message (IM) names.

FIGURE 3.3 You can use the Search for People feature to look for people you know on Facebook.

> **Tip**
> You can click the **Invite Friends** link on the left side of the page to invite people you know to join Facebook. When you click the link, a message form appears that you can fill out and email to people you want to invite.

To search for someone on Facebook, just click in the text box under the Search for People area of the page and type in a name; then click the **Search** button or press the **Enter** or **Return** key. Facebook displays a results page with any matches, similar to Figure 3.4. Depending on how common the name is, you may have to scroll through and view each match to determine if it's the right person or not. If in doubt, you can always send an email message inquiring whether it's the person you think you know or not using the **Send a Message** link.

FIGURE 3.4 When you conduct a search, Facebook displays a results page with possible matches. It's up to you to figure out who exactly you're looking for.

From the results page, you can click the **Profile Search** link at the top and conduct a more detailed search based on profile information. If you click the **Friend Finder** link, the same Friends page information opens again as shown in Figure 3.2.

> **Tip**
>
> To search for AOL Instant Messenger or Windows Live Messenger buddies, choose a link under the Find People You IM area of the Friends page. You can look up people you contact using instant messaging.

You can also conduct a search for someone using the **Search** field at the top of the Facebook page on the blue navigation bar.

When you do finally find a friend on Facebook, you can send him or her a friend request by clicking the **Add as Friend** link. When you click the link, a box pops up, shown in Figure 3.5. Facebook lets you know that the person will have to confirm you as his or her friend first. You can use the box to add a personal message to the request. You can also choose to categorize the friend if you have organized your friends into lists (learn more about this later in the chapter).

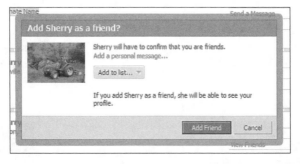

FIGURE 3.5 You have the option of sending a personal message along with your friend request.

> **Tip**
>
> When you add a new friend, you can use Facebook's friend suggestion feature to connect the person to other friends you both know. This feature is especially helpful if your friend is new to Facebook. Open the person's profile page and scroll down a bit under his or her profile picture to find the **Suggest Friends for** link. Click it to open a box for selecting friends to suggest and send along to the people you think might be interested in knowing the new friend.

Responding to Friends Who Find You

While you're busy inviting people to be your friend, don't forget to look
for friend requests from other people. When you're the lucky recipient of
an invitation from another Facebook user, it appears on your Home page
as a friend request up in the requests area. Facebook also alerts you
with an email if you've turned on the requests feature. In the top-right
corner of the Home page, shown in Figure 3.6, Facebook lists any notifications you have waiting to deal with, such as friend requests or event
invitations.

FIGURE 3.6   Remember to check your requests area for requests and invitations.

Click the **friend requests** link to open the Requests page, shown in Figure
3.7, which lists all kinds of requests, including invitations for joining
groups, causes, responding to party invites, game challenges, and more.

FIGURE 3.7   The Requests page keeps a running list of all your requests,
including friend requests.

If you're having trouble remembering who the person is or how you might
know him, you can click his picture to view his profile first, and then
decide to add him as a friend or not. You can also click the **mutual friends**
link and learn which mutual friends you have in common. If you're still
having trouble figuring out who the person is, you can click the **Send
Message** link and fire off an email message—perhaps to diplomatically
authenticate that it's the person you think it is, or maybe just to say hello.

If you've organized your friends into lists (which is covered in the next
section), you can choose to categorize the person to a particular list using
the **Add to list** pop-up menu before you actually confirm him as a friend.

If you decide you'd rather not befriend the person on Facebook, you can click the **Ignore** link. This makes the request disappear without approval.

To process a friend request and make it official, you can simply click the **Confirm** link next to the person's picture, as shown in Figure 3.7. Facebook immediately adds the person to your friends list and gives you options for suggesting new friends, adding details about the friend, or writing on the person's wall, as shown in Figure 3.8.

FIGURE 3.8   Facebook displays this information immediately after you confirm a friend request.

Viewing and Editing Friends

After you start accumulating friends on Facebook, you'll want to view their profiles from time to time and see what they're up to online, or check out their latest photo or video postings. For starters, when you open your profile page, Facebook displays a random list of friends in a little Friends box area on the left side of the page. You can click a friend to view his or her profile. There are far more ways to view as well. The best place to begin is on the Friends page. The Friends page offers all kinds of ways to view, filter, and organize your friends on Facebook.

Tip

All the box areas on your profile page are editable, including the Friends box. Just click the **Edit** button—the button that looks like a tiny pencil icon—in the upper-right corner of the area and choose an option. In the case of the Edit box for friends, you can choose to increase or decrease the number of friends displayed in the area, or choose to show only certain friends.

Viewing Friends

There are several routes you can take to the Friends page. You've already learned how to open the Friends page to the search options earlier in this lesson. Now you'll learn how to view your friends list. You can click the **Friends** link on the Facebook navigation bar at the top of the page and then click **All Friends**. You can also hover the mouse pointer over the **Friends** link and click **All Friends**. In addition, you can also click the **See All** link found in the Friends box area on your profile page and then click **All Friends**. Any of these paths will take you to a page displaying your list of friends, similar to Figure 3.9.

FIGURE 3.9 The friends list is simply a page or pages listing all your Facebook friends.

To view any friend's profile in the list, just click the person's name or photo. There are a couple of filters you can use on the left side to filter the list and show recently added friends, or friends who have updated their status. You can click the **Browse** link, for example, to browse friends based on their network.

If your friends have added phone information to their profiles, such as a cell phone number, you can click the **Phonebook** link and view their contact information.

Organizing Friends into Lists

If you like organization, you'll love Facebook's friend lists. You can group your friends into lists, which is particularly useful if you have hundreds of them on Facebook. For example, you may have a list for family and another for close friends, and still another list filled with casual acquaintances. Lists can help you keep track of different groups at different times, or send out messages to everyone in a group all at once.

If you're like most people, you probably talk about some subjects with everybody and other subjects with only those who are close to you. For example, you may freely express your political or religious views, but not everyone on your friends list or network may want to share in those views. So you end up having private conversations with some, and more public conversations with others. You can make sure your separate worlds don't collide on Facebook using friend lists as a tool for communicating and organizing.

To create a friend list, follow these steps:

1. Navigate to the Friends page and click **All Friends**.

2. Click the **Create List** button at the top of the lists area.

3. In the Create New List box (see Figure 3.10), type a name for the new list and press **Enter** or **Return**.

4. You can scroll through and click on people you want to add to the new list, or you can type their names in the field at the top of the box.

5. When you finish adding friends to the list, click the **Create List** button.

After you create a new list, Facebook saves it and displays the Home page showing only the status updates and news feed of the people on the list you just made. To return to the normal news feed again that shows all your friends, just click the **News Feed** link on the upper-left side of the Home page. Anytime you want to view the news feed with just the friends from the list you created, just click its name on the Home page. You can also click the list name from your Friends page.

FIGURE 3.10   You can use the Create New List box to whip up a specialized list of Facebook friends.

You can easily add names to a list, or remove names. The list is just for you; no one else can see your lists. To edit your list, return to the Friends page and click the list. Click the **Edit List** button and make your changes. When you finish, click the **Save List** button.

To remove a list entirely, display the list and click the **Delete List** button; then click **Delete List** from the box that appears.

You can use Facebook's emailing features to email everyone on a list all at once. To learn more about sending messages in Facebook, see Lesson 7, "Communicating Through Facebook."

Un-Friending Friends

As your friends list grows, you may encounter an occasion in which you want to "un-friend" someone. For example, if the person turns out to be a notorious spammer or you have a falling out of some kind, you can remove the person from your list, or perhaps you want to pare down your list to just people you actually know in some way. There's no official declaration of this action; however, if your friend goes looking for you in her friend list, your name won't appear anymore.

To remove a friend, display his or her profile page and click the **Remove from Friends** link located near the bottom-left area of the page. You can also click the person's name on your Friends page friends list (see Figure 3.9) and click the **X** button to the right of the person's name. A prompt box appears, as shown in Figure 3.11. Click the **Remove** button to finalize the removal.

FIGURE 3.11   A friend removal action is permanent.

There's no undo button for a friend removal. If you do want to "re-friend" them again at a later time, you'll have to beg them to be your friend again through a friend request.

Summary

In this lesson, you learned how to join a network, look for friends on Facebook, and respond to friend requests. You also learned how to view your friend list and organize your friends into other lists. Finally, you learned how to "un-friend" a friend. In the next lesson, you learn how to use Facebook's Help Center and find some tips for conducting yourself on the website.

LESSON 4

Finding Help with Facebook Services and Etiquette

In this lesson, you learn about Facebook's terms of service, what to expect with the social do's and don'ts of using Facebook, and how to find help with the website.

Understanding Facebook's Terms of Service

Facebook operates under the guidance of a set of values, goals, and rules for how the site works and how the users interact. These guidelines are important for the general well-being of its members, as well as the smooth and seamless function of the site. When you sign up for Facebook, you're agreeing to uphold and follow their terms of service. If you're like most people, however, you didn't take time to read all the legalese and fine print. In a nutshell, the terms of service are broken down into several categories, such as privacy, information sharing, safety, account security, and topics along those lines.

You can read the terms yourself by scrolling to the bottom of any Facebook page and clicking the **Terms** link. The link always sits at the bottom of a page, along with links to Facebook's Help page and privacy principles. When you click the Terms link, Facebook opens a page detailing a statement of rights and responsibilities, as shown in Figure 4.1.

FIGURE 4.1   Facebook's terms of service page.

You can certainly take time to read all the fine print, but if you just want a quick overview, here are a few details about the terms that you need to follow:

Privacy   Facebook promises to do their best to keep your information private or at least disclose to you if they share it with others. It's up to you to control your own privacy settings, however. (Learn more about changing privacy settings in Lesson 5.)

Sharing Content and Information   You're the owner of the content and information you post on Facebook; however, by posting it, you're giving Facebook permission to use any content covered by intellectual property rights, kind of a license to use the content until you cancel your account.

Note

Keep in mind that if you delete content or even your entire Facebook account, much of that content still resides somewhere on the servers. For this reason, do not post content that you do not want others to access or control.

Safety   Under this broad category, you cannot collect information from other users, send spam, upload viruses, solicit login information from others, bully other users, or use Facebook for illegal purposes. In other words, behave yourself.

Content   You cannot post content that is hateful or threatening to others. You cannot post pornographic material, or nudity of any kind. You're also not allowed to post anything featuring gratuitous violence. This terms of service category is basically about using common sense and being a good citizen, conducting yourself in a way that would make your parents proud.

Account Security   You cannot supply Facebook with false or outdated information, and it's up to you to keep your password safe and prevent unauthorized access. You cannot use Facebook if you're under 13 years of age. You cannot use Facebook if you're in a country that is currently under embargo. If you're a convicted sex offender, you're not allowed on Facebook.

So what happens if you violate the terms of service? Facebook has the right to terminate your account for any misdeeds, misconduct, illegal activities, and so forth. They can remove questionable content you post if it violates the terms of service. Basically, you'll get in trouble if you don't play nicely with others. Most of us learned this concept early on; however, there's always someone out there looking for trouble. If you encounter such a person, you can report them on Facebook (see Lesson 5, "Guarding Your Privacy," to learn more).

If you're interested in reading more about Facebook's privacy policies, such as exactly what information is collected from you and shared, click the **Privacy** link at the bottom of any Facebook page. You can also get to the page by clicking the **Privacy Policy** link found amidst the terms of service information.

Like many large-scale websites, Facebook's terms and privacy policies change over time. You can always revisit the terms of service and principles pages to read up about the most current rules and regulations.

Facebook Etiquette

As you can probably guess, anytime you throw together a bunch of people from diverse backgrounds, ages, experiences, political leanings, religions, and computer proficiency, things happen—expectations differ, assumptions are made, worlds collide. Just like interacting in the real world, interacting in the online world takes some skill and diplomacy. Sure, you may have joined Facebook just to have fun with your friends, but maybe your version of fun differs from the people you have assembled on your Friends List. So what are the social do's and don'ts of using Facebook?

There's no real guide to interacting other than your own common sense and intuition. As in real life, in online life, the golden rule still applies—treat others as you want to be treated. If you're looking for a few tips anyway, here they are.

Facebook Do's

Do be tolerant of others, particularly when you get friend requests from people you don't immediately recognize or know. They may be looking for someone with the same name. If you don't want to respond, just ignore the request.

Do set your privacy settings to the levels in which you feel comfortable and safe. By default, many of the privacy settings are set for everyone to see your profile information and other postings. It's a good idea to adjust these settings to include just your friends. (See Lesson 5 to learn more about Facebook settings.)

Do report threatening behavior or inappropriate postings. Facebook takes this sort of thing very seriously. You can visit the Help page to find a report feature.

Do be considerate of other people's feelings. Communicating electronically is often a challenge because people can't see your face or hear the tone of your voice. Remember this when posting on Walls and making comments.

Do reply to Wall comments and personal messages when applicable. It's mannerly to at least acknowledge people who attempt to communicate with you.

Do keep your Wall postings civil and free of foul or questionable language. Remember, that person's other friends see your comments, including the possibility of that person's mother.

Do choose an appropriate profile picture. Tacky or questionable pictures are not the way to go unless that's really the message you want to convey to friends, family, coworkers, or your boss.

Do use your head about what information you share on Facebook and how you conduct yourself. When it comes to the issue of saying too much online, let discretion be your first instinct. It's always better to say too little than too much.

Facebook Don'ts

Don't think of your friends list as a competition to see who has the most. It's not. Quality over quantity is the best approach. If you're sending friend requests right and left to people you don't intend to know, you're in this for the wrong reasons.

Don't give out your personal information unless you really know the person, and rely on private email messages, not the public forum that is the Facebook Wall. Always be cautious about sharing personal or confidential information—never give out your information to someone you don't know.

Don't irritate people with your postings. Keep in mind that not everyone wants to hear about your pet rabbit every single hour of every single day.

Don't annoy people with too many "pokes" or other application actions. It's fun the first time, but over and over again all day is too much. (See Lesson 12, "Adding Applications," to learn more about applications.)

Don't use Facebook as a tool for revenge, bullying, or threats. Such activities will get you kicked off faster than a speeding bullet.

Don't feel obligated to befriend everyone on Facebook. If you don't want a particular person snooping around your profile, you can deny their friend request.

Don't share company information online—that's a big no-no.

Don't make your romantic break-ups and get-togethers public knowledge. Save that sort of information for private forums.

Don't lower your guard just because you're with "friends" on Facebook. Accounts can be hijacked, and shared links can take you to questionable places or encourage you to download files that turn out to be viruses or malware.

Finding Help with the Help Center

You may encounter times in which you need a little extra help with your Facebook experience—for example, if you're having a technical issue with your account or want to know more about a particular feature. Check out the Facebook Help Center for answers. The Help Center, shown in Figure 4.2, is just a click away. To view the page, click the **Help** link at the bottom of any Facebook page.

FIGURE 4.2 Visit Facebook's Help Center page when you need help.

The Help Center page offers three tabs: Help Center, Getting Started, and Safety. By default, the Help Center tab is displayed, as shown in Figure 4.2. Help Center topics are grouped into sections on this page. To read more about a topic, just click it to open a page with more details. If you don't find the answer you're looking for, try clicking another topic.

To look up a topic, click in the **Search** box at the top of the Help Center page, type in the word or phrase you want to look up, and press **Enter**.

The Top Searches box in the upper-right corner keeps a running display of current top search topics conducted by Facebook users.

Click the **Getting Started** tab, shown in Figure 4.3, to view three tutorials you can read to learn more about finding friends, setting up a profile, and exploring the website.

FIGURE 4.3   You can find some tutorials about using Facebook on the Getting Started tab.

Finally, the **Safety** tab has information about Facebook's safety policies and how to keep yourself online. The info includes a list of frequently asked questions, tips for parents of children on Facebook, and links to other sites offering safety information.

Tip

If you're still having trouble finding help, try one of the many blogs focused on Facebook, including http://blog.facebook.com or www.all-facebook.com. If you're an advertiser on Facebook, the Inside Facebook blog is worth checking out at www.insidefacebook.com. If you're having a technical issue, try the People-powered Customer Service for Facebook board at http://getsatisfaction.com/facebook.

Summary

In this lesson, you learned about Facebook's terms of service, a few tips for following proper social networking etiquette, and how to find help in times of trouble using Facebook's Help Center pages. In the next lesson, you learn how to utilize the privacy settings to control who has access to your information.

LESSON 5

Guarding Your Privacy

In this lesson, you learn how to protect yourself on Facebook by logging on more smartly, changing your privacy settings, and learning how to keep yourself safe.

Understanding Privacy and Security Settings on Facebook

Privacy and security are the number-one concerns on the Internet, and are particularly relevant in the world of social networking. Identity theft is growing daily and spammers lurk behind every website trying to nab your email address. It's more important than ever to guard yourself online. Along with these dangers, a social networking site like Facebook also throws in the risks of humiliation, embarrassment, and criticism if you end up posting information you're not supposed to or revealing far too much information to the wrong people. So how do you begin to protect yourself and still network freely?

The reality is anything you post on Facebook has the potential to be publicly available. This includes your picture and your profile information, such as political views, relationship status, and so on. Facebook does do all it can to protect your personal information, but things happen, hackers can attack, and so on. It's easy to think that only people you allow to be your friends on Facebook can view your info, but that's not the case. There are ways of finding someone's profile on Facebook. Potential employers, law enforcement, teachers, and anyone else determined to do so can find a way to see your profile. If your privacy settings are lax, even a simple search engine can access your profile.

Companies and third-party developers that partner with Facebook can also access your information when allowed. Per Facebook's policy, advertisers who sell products on Facebook can access your information, so it's up to those companies to also safeguard the info. There are hundreds of third-party applications available on Facebook, and to make use of them, you must allow them access to your information. In doing so, there is the potential for unscrupulous third-party developers to misuse your data. Because you've allowed them access to the info by adding the application to your account, there's not much Facebook can do about it.

The bottom line is it's up to you to take steps to protect yourself. Thankfully, there are some strategies you can pursue to help battle privacy and security breaches, and stop them before they ever occur.

Pursuing Protection Strategies

Despite the possibilities for exposure and risk, don't let the fear of privacy and security keep you from enjoying your Facebook experience. You can keep yourself relatively safe just by following a few simple practices:

- ▶ First and foremost—use common sense when participating in any online endeavor. If something seems risky, it probably is. If someone from your Facebook network emails you about a get-rich plan, you can be sure it's a scam, so don't take the bait.

- ▶ Never give out personal or sensitive information in a public forum. For example, don't post your cell phone number so it can be read in everyone's Facebook newsfeed. You're just asking for trouble.

- ▶ If a Facebook user stalks you or harasses you, you can block their access to your profile and report them to Facebook.

- ▶ Although the profile information form (see Lesson 2, "Setting Up a Profile") has places for it, you're not required to place personal information of any kind in your profile. For example, if you don't feel comfortable adding your home or work address and phone numbers, don't do it. You can share this type of information through a private email on a "need-to-know" basis.

► If you're worried about spammers, consider using a free email address from a site like Google or Yahoo! for your Facebook account. This can help you protect your main email address from unwanted exposure.

► Always be leery of links to sites outside of Facebook that come to you via friends. Make sure the site is legitimate before giving out information. *Phishing*, the practice of tricking people into revealing sensitive data, is widespread, but you can usually spot these threats by their poor grammar and typos, so keep your eyes peeled.

► Even though Facebook advocates honesty, people aren't always what or who they seem to be online. Be skeptical, cautious, and vigilant when it comes to meeting new people online.

► When it comes to deciding whether to post something or not, just ask yourself if your mom or your employer would be comfortable with it. For example, do you really want your mom or your boss to see a picture of you at that wild party last weekend? Better to err on the side of good judgment when it comes to your personal information and pictures.

► Finally, make use of the controls Facebook offers to help you stay safe on the site. Why let useful privacy control settings go to waste?

The rest of this lesson shows you practical steps you can take to protect your privacy and security on Facebook.

Controlling Account Access

The best way to control your Facebook account is to use some smart logon practices. When you log onto your account from the top of the main Facebook page, shown in Figure 5.1, you have the option of checking the **Remember me** check box. This feature tells Facebook to keep you logged on until you decide to log out using the **Logout** link. Although this may seem like a handy way to avoid typing in your ID and password each time you access your account, it's actually a problem if you're using Facebook on a shared computer. For example, if you're using a computer at a public library, school, or workplace, other users access the computer after you. If you forget to log out, the next user at the computer can access your account. In other words, you've left the door to your information wide open.

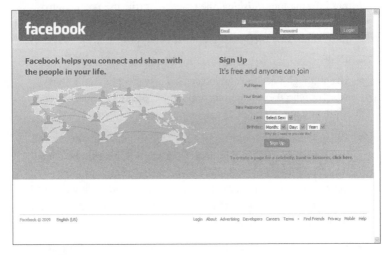

FIGURE 5.1   Facebook's logon page.

To prevent unwanted access, make sure the **Remember me** check box is deselected when you log onto your account. Secondly, always log off the site when you're finished by clicking the **Logout** link at the top of the web page.

Customizing Your Privacy Settings

By default, the Facebook privacy settings are often set to their lowest levels unless you specify otherwise. For example, your photos are automatically viewable by everyone on Facebook when you publish them unless you change the setting. You can quickly turn some controls on or off using

the Facebook Privacy pages. Log onto Facebook and move your mouse
pointer over the **Settings** link at the top of the Facebook page; then click
the **Privacy Settings** option from the pop-up menu that appears (see
Figure 5.2).

FIGURE 5.2   Access privacy settings through the Settings menu.

Facebook displays the Privacy page, similar to Figure 5.3. The page features links to controlling privacy settings for your profile, how you appear
to others in Facebook's search tools, news feed and wall, applications, and
a member block list.

FIGURE 5.3   The Privacy Settings page.

> **Tip**
>
> If you're worried about people seeing your picture on your Facebook profile, consider using an image other than an actual photo of you. For example, you might use a picture related to your hobbies or interests instead. Visit Lesson 2 to learn more about adding and changing a profile picture.

Controlling Profile Privacy

To edit your profile privacy settings, click the **Profile** link on the Privacy page. You can also click the **Manage** link in the Privacy category on the My Account page, and then click the **Profile** link. Facebook opens a page with two tabs full of settings: Basic and Contact Information. From the Basic tab, shown in Figure 5.4, you can control who sees your profile. Use the Contact Information tab to control who sees your contact information.

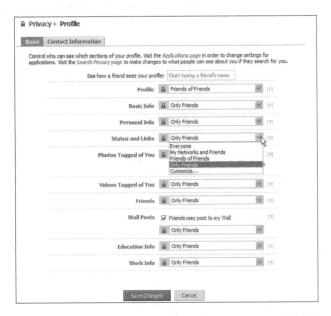

FIGURE 5.4 The Basic tab lets you control who sees your profile information.

To see what everyone else sees when they look at your profile, you can click in the text box at the top of the Basic tab and type a friend's name. When you complete the name or select it from the list that appears, Facebook shows you what that particular user sees on your profile. You can click the **Back** button on your browser window to return to the Basic tab again and change what appears on the profile page.

To change who sees your profile, click the **Profile** drop-down menu and choose an option: **Everyone**, **Friends of Friends**, or **Only Friends**. If you're on a network, the list includes **My Networks and Friends** and **Customize**. The Customize option opens a dialog box, shown in Figure 5.5, that lets you specify which networks and types of friends on those networks view your info.

FIGURE 5.5 The Customize dialog box lets you specify exactly which networks can view your info.

After you edit any of the Basic settings, click the **Save Changes** button at the bottom of the tab to save your work. If you don't, the new settings won't take effect.

You can click the **Contact Information** tab, shown in Figure 5.6, to view settings for controlling who sees your contact information, such as your cell phone or address. Like the settings in the Basic tab, you can click a drop-down menu and choose a privacy setting for each contact item. Click the **Save Changes** button to keep any new settings you specify.

FIGURE 5.6   Use the Contact Information tab to control who can view your contact information.

It's up to you to decide how much of your data is viewable. Take time to look through all the settings and choose which levels best suit your Facebook usage.

Controlling Searches

From the Privacy page (see Figure 5.3), you can click the **Search** option and control who can search for you on Facebook and what information they see in the search results. The Search page, shown in Figure 5.7, lets you control your visibility on Facebook searches and specify exactly which information in your profile they can view, such as your friend list or fan pages. There's also a setting for allowing outside search engines to access your profile.

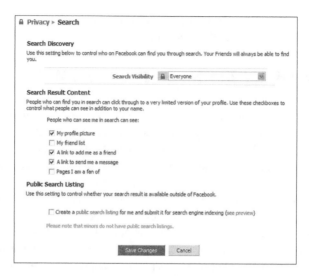

FIGURE 5.7 The Search settings let you control how people search for you on Facebook and outside of Facebook.

If you've set the Search Visibility setting to Everyone, then the Public Search Listing section appears. If you want to allow outside search engines, like Google, to access your Facebook listing, click the check box under the Public Search Listing area. You can click the **see preview** link to see what the search results look like. For full privacy, however, it is recommended that you not select this option.

> **Note**
>
> If you're a minor, your Facebook information will not be available in a public search regardless of whether you click the check box in the Public Search Listing area or not.

If you still want people to find you online in Facebook, consider setting the **Search Visibility** setting to **Everyone**, but limit what they can see in the search result content. This approach allows old friends and acquaintances the opportunity to look you up without revealing too much information about yourself.

Finally, to keep all the new settings you changed on this page, click the
Save Changes button at the bottom of the page.

Controlling the News Feed and Wall

Facebook tracks your activities on the site, such as Wall posts and com-
ments, and reports them in an ongoing, scrollable news feed that appears
on the Home page. You can control how your actions are tracked using the
News Feed and Wall privacy settings. Back to the Privacy page again (see
Figure 5.3), you can click the **News Feed and Wall** option to view the
controls shown in Figure 5.8. This page has two tabs: Actions within
Facebook and Social Ads. The Actions within Facebook tab, shown in
Figure 5.8, lets you control which activities you perform are visible to the
rest of the Facebook community. You can turn off your Wall posting activities, for example, or turn off all the commenting activities you pursue
regularly. Whether you've noticed yet or not, even your profile edits, such
as changing your relationship status, appear on the news feed and Wall.
You can turn off the tracking of these activities as well.

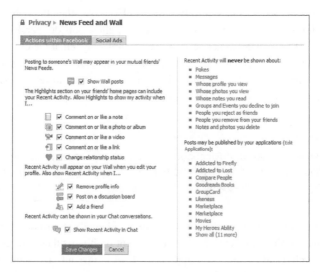

FIGURE 5.8   The Actions within Facebook tab lets you control which activities appear on the news feed and your Wall.

As you can see in the figure, the left side of the tab has check boxes for controlling activity appearance, whereas the right side lists what activities appear or don't appear. To make changes to the settings, just deselect or select the appropriate check boxes. When you finish with your edits, click the **Save Changes** button at the bottom of the tab page.

If you buy something or become a fan of a page based on a social ad, Facebook displays the activity, and your name or avatar appears in that ad for your friends to see. You can opt out of this. Click the **Social Ads** tab click the pop-up menu, and select **No one**. Click the **Save Changes** button, and you're done.

Controlling Applications

Applications are add-on programs that work with Facebook. They come in a wide variety of types and functions, from the serious to the silly. Some applications, or *apps* for short, are part of your Facebook account by default, such as the Notes and Photos applications. We'll cover applications in greater detail in Lesson 12, "Adding Applications," but as it relates to privacy, let's talk about how to control them a bit here so you're better informed when more apps start crossing your path later.

Here's a fact—most of the applications you add in Facebook access your profile information. You typically can't use an application unless you allow this. Sounds logical, yes? But did you know that applications your friends allow access to can also access information about you just because you're their friend? Sneaky, eh? You can deauthorize this access using the Applications page as part of the Facebook privacy settings. You can also control what types of information are shared. To find your way to the Applications privacy settings, click the **Applications** link on the Privacy page (see Figure 5.3). The page offers two tabs: Overview and Settings. The Overview tab spells out exactly how applications interact with your Facebook information. Take a minute to read up on this; you may find it to be very interesting. Among the fine print are links to changing some of the other privacy settings you've already learned about in this lesson.

To control how the applications use your info, click the **Settings** tab, shown in Figure 5.9. Here you can specify what information is shared, link to the Applications Setting page, turn off Facebook Connect Applications and Beacon Websites, and more.

For complete privacy, you can select the **Do not share** option at the bottom of the group of check boxes, or you can deselect all but a few of the check boxes. As long as we're making everything private, you should also select the **Don't allow** options for the Facebook Connect Applications check box and the Beacon Websites check box. Facebook Connect uses applications outside the Facebook environment to share information on the Internet. Beacon is Facebook's advertising program and, when allowed, it submits stories to your news feed about your outside activities, such as purchasing concert or movie tickets through an online source. If you don't want to share such information, opt out of both options.

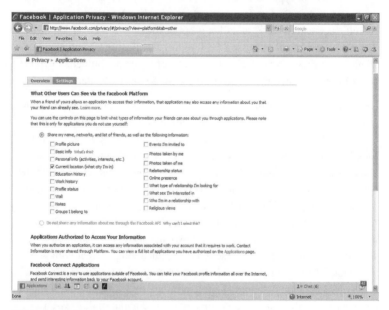

FIGURE 5.9 The Settings tab lets you control what information applications can access.

To control applications themselves, you must visit the Application Settings page, shown in Figure 5.10. To find your way to this page, click the **Settings** link at the top of the Facebook page and then click **Application Settings**. You can also click the **Applications** link on the Applications Privacy Settings page.

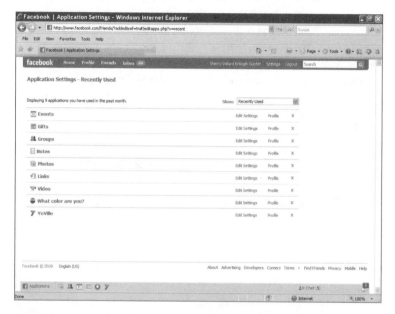

FIGURE 5.10 The Application Settings page keeps a running list of your Facebook applications.

From the list of applications, you can edit the settings, read more about the application itself, or remove it entirely.

Click the **Edit Settings** link to open a dialog box of controls for the application where you can further fine-tune how the app works with your information.

Click the **About** link to learn more about the app, its author, and which friends are using it.

To remove an application entirely, click the **X** button and click **Remove**. You'll be prompted when the process is over; click **Okay**.

To learn more about applications and how they work in Facebook, see
Lesson 12.

Blocking People

The final topic to cover under Facebook's privacy controls is how to block
other Facebook members. On the Privacy page, shown in Figure 5.11, a
whole area on the page is sectioned off for this topic. This particular feature is used to block someone from bothering you or accessing you on
Facebook. When you block them, they can no longer see your profile
information or interact with you through Facebook features. This also
means you can no longer see them on Facebook either. Blocking them
only knocks them out of contacting you in Facebook. Outside of
Facebook is another matter.

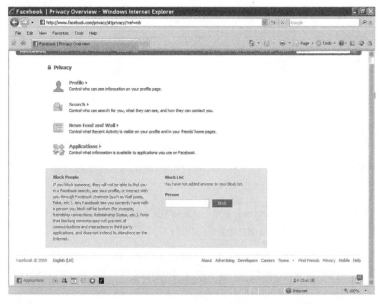

FIGURE 5.11   Use the Block People area to block other Facebook members.

To block someone, simply type their name in the text box and click the
Block button. You can then identify exactly who you're trying to block

from a list of matches, and narrow it down to the right person. Click the
Block Person button next to their name, and the deed is done.

> **Tip**
>
> You can unblock a person you've previously blocked. Just return to
> the Privacy Settings page and unblock them in your list. You'll have
> to "re-friend" them again to include them back in your network or
> friends list.

Reporting Abuse

Facebook tries to maintain a safe environment, but like the real world, the
online world is often fraught with illegal, offensive, and inappropriate
material and conduct. Nudity, pornography, harassment, hate speech, and
unwelcome contact is against the rules. If you spot something along these
lines, you can report it to Facebook. To contact them directly, you can
email abuse@facebook.com, and they'll look into the problem. In addition
to this route, you can find **Report** links scattered throughout the Facebook
pages. You can click a link to report a problem. For example, if you
encounter a pornographic picture in someone's photo album, you can
click the **Report This Photo** link.

You can check out Facebook's Security page for more help with questionable material and conduct and how to find help. To access the page, click
the **Help** link at the bottom of any Facebook page to open the Help
Center; then click the **Security** link to view related links. You can also
click the **Safety** tab on the Help Center page to learn more.

> **Tip**
>
> Anytime you want to refresh your knowledge of Facebook's Terms of
> Service, click the **Terms** link at the bottom of any Facebook page.
> This opens a page with information, links to privacy settings, and
> so on.

Summary

In this lesson, you learned all about Facebook's privacy settings and how to keep your data safe while using the website. In the next lesson, you learn how to work with news feeds and manage your scrolling Wall.

LESSON 6

Tracking Wall Postings, News Feeds, and Notifications

In this lesson, you learn how to keep track of news and activities on Facebook. You'll learn how information flows on the site, and how to manage your Wall, news feed, and notifications to keep abreast of the latest information.

Understanding Facebook Information Flow

As a social networking site, Facebook acts much like a broadcasting service, sharing news about its members wherever they are. However, rather than tuning in to see general news about everyone on the site or stories selected entirely by Facebook, your news is narrowed down to just the people you know—your friends, family, coworkers, or colleagues. The news that is shared, whether it's status updates, photos, or the latest group someone joined, is referred to as *stories* on Facebook. This news is also called feed stories or news feed stories. The information that appears on the Home page is a constant stream of stories about the activities and pursuits of your friends. The official name for this is *news feeds*. The stories that appear on your profile are called *mini-feeds* because they're all about you.

For example, anytime you post a status update on your Wall, it's a story on your mini-feed—information dedicated to you. When your friend shares a photo, for example, it appears on his Wall as a mini-feed about him. Out on the Home page, both stories may appear listed as news feed stories where other friends you both know can see.

What exactly constitutes as *news* on Facebook, you may wonder? Anything you do on the site is considered a story. If you join a group, for example, or share a link, it appears as part of your mini-feed, as well as potentially listed in the main news feed. If you don't want to share all your Facebook activities, you can turn off some of this through your privacy settings (see Lesson 5, "Guarding Your Privacy," to learn more).

Another part of this ongoing stream of broadcasting is a Facebook feature called *notifications*. Notifications are messages from Facebook telling you about something that happened on Facebook involving you somehow, such as being tagged (pointed out) in a photo or if someone wrote on your Wall. Your Facebook notifications appear on the Notifications pop-up list, or they arrive in your Inbox and appear in the Notifications tab. Unlike mini-feeds that are generated by you, or news feeds that detail the activities of others, notifications involve you indirectly. Depending on your settings, some notifications are also sent to your email address.

Let's get down to the nitty-gritty details of how to manage your mini-feeds, news feeds, and notifications.

Managing Your Wall

The Wall on your profile page is your public forum for communicating with your Facebook friends and they, in turn, with you. The Wall is a big part of your profile page, located smack-dab in the middle of the page. You can use your Wall to share comments and musings, photos and videos, links to interesting sites, and more. Anytime you update your status, the information appears on your Wall. Friends who view your page can also write on your Wall, or comment on your existing postings. This ongoing spot for social commentary is essentially a mini-feed of news focused solely on you. The news items you post on your Wall, whether it's text or links or photos, are interchangeably called *stories* on Facebook. Figure 6.1 shows an example of a typical Wall. The Wall appears by default when you display your profile. If, by chance, you've clicked another tab on your profile page instead, you can click the **Wall** tab to return to the Wall view at any time.

FIGURE 6.1   Use the Wall to share information, such as what you're currently doing, postings of your favorite video clips, and more.

As you add new information onto your Wall, previous postings scroll down to make room for the latest items at the top. You can use your browser window's scroll bar on the right to scroll up and down your Wall stories. Based on how much you or your friends add to your Wall, the postings may change hourly, daily, or weekly. You can use the **Show Older Posts** link at the bottom of your Wall to view older postings. The more you log on and interact on Facebook, the more activities show up on your Wall. There are lots of things you can do to work with and manage your Wall. This section shows you how.

Tip

You can adjust privacy settings for your Wall and news feed activities. Move your mouse pointer over the **Settings** link at the top of the Facebook page and click **Privacy Settings** to open the Privacy page. Click the **News Feed and Wall** link to view your options.

Updating Your Status

To post something on your own Wall, fill out a status update and share it. Essentially, this creates a story on your page. Click in the text box at the top of your profile page, as shown in Figure 6.2, where it says something like "**What's on your mind?**." In previous versions of the Facebook interface, the box had different titles; the name or text may change at any-time, but the intent remains the same—to share something that you're thinking or doing, some random remark, observation, or witty thought. Type out your status update; then click the **Share** button to post it on your page. Facebook adds the information to your Wall, as well as to the news feed that appears on your Home page and your friend's Home pages.

FIGURE 6.2   Use the status update box to post an update about what you're doing or thinking.

Tip
You can also fill out the update box on your Home page to update your Facebook status.

The update box is technically known as the Publisher. When you activate the **What's on your mind?** box, which you can do just by clicking inside the field, the Facebook Publisher displays additional buttons below the field for sharing a link, photo, or video along with your comment text. If you have other applications loaded, you can click the arrow button at the end of the row of buttons and add an application action to the comment as well. If you click the **Link** button, for example, you can add a link to another web page to share along with your comment. To learn more about sharing links, see Lesson 7, "Communicating Through Facebook." To learn how to share photos, see Lesson 8, "Sharing Photos." To learn how to share videos, see Lesson 9, "Sharing Videos."

How often you update your status is entirely up to you. It really depends on how often you log onto Facebook and how much you want to share about what you're doing or thinking. Some users like to post updates several times a day; others like to post more sporadically based on things that happen throughout their day. Other users like to update their status once a day or, if feeling not so social, once a week. Facebook Walls are really all about connecting with your friends, so it's up to you to decide how much to participate and share.

Removing Wall Postings

There may be times in which you need to edit your Wall postings—for example, you may have misspelled a word or need to remove a questionable posting a friend left on your Wall. You can remove the story with the error and replace it with a corrected version. To remove a posting or story, point to the item on the Wall to display a tiny **Remove** button to the far right of the posting. Click the button to open a Delete Post box, as shown in Figure 6.3. Click the **Delete** button to confirm the removal.

Delete Post

Are you sure you want to delete this post?

Delete   Cancel

Sherry   Matty bought me some new chicks

FIGURE 6.3   You can easily remove a posting from your Wall.

> **Tip**
>
> If removing postings from a particular person is a pain, consider adjusting your privacy settings to prevent future postings. Move your mouse pointer over the **Settings** link at the top of the Facebook page and click **Privacy Settings**; then click the **Profile** link on the Privacy page that appears. Next, click the pop-up menu under **Wall Posts** and choose **Customize**. This opens a dialog box where you can type in the name of the person who is no longer allowed to post to your Wall.

Filtering Your Wall Postings

You may notice three blue words at the top of the Wall: *YourName* + Friends, Just *YourName*, and Just Friends. If you don't see the filter options, click the **Options** link located below the status update box. These are filters that control what's displayed on the Wall. By default, the Wall displays postings by both you and your friends. You can choose to filter the postings by displaying just your own postings, or viewing only the postings left by friends. Simply click a filter name at the top of the Wall, as shown in Figure 6.4. Facebook immediately shows the postings based on your selection. To return to the default setting again, click the first filter (*YourName* + Friends). Filters only apply to your view of your Wall, not your friend's view of your Wall.

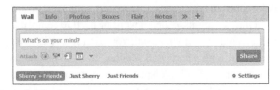

FIGURE 6.4   Use the filters to filter your Wall postings.

You can use these same filtering tools on your friends' Walls. When you open a friend's profile page, you can click the **Filters** link to display the same filter buttons. Of course, instead of your name on the buttons, the friend's name appears.

Writing on a Friend's Wall

You saw how easy it is to write on your own Wall by posting a status update with the Publisher box. You can also post comments on your friends' Walls. Start by displaying a friend's profile page. You can do this from a variety of pages, such as the Home page or friends list, just by clicking on your friend's name link. After her profile is open, click in the **Write something** box, as shown in Figure 6.5, and type your text. Oddly enough, it's the same box you use to update the status on your own profile page, just featuring a slightly different label. As soon as you click the **Share** button, the comment is added to her profile page and also appears on the Home page as one of your activities.

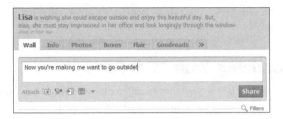

FIGURE 6.5   You can write on your friend's Wall using the Write something text box.

If you'd prefer to add to something someone else has already written instead, just click the **Comment** link below the posting and add your two cents, or click in the **Write a comment** box and type in your comment text. You can also comment on your own postings on your own profile page. When you add a comment, it appears beneath the original story item. If lots of people comment to a story, you can scroll down the comments and see what everyone says. Sometimes entire conversations unfold under just one story posting.

Tip

If you don't have time to type up a text comment, you can always signify your approval of the story by clicking the **Like** link instead. This adds a thumbs-up icon to the story along with your name.

Viewing Wall-to-Wall Conversations

One aspect of communicating via Walls is the appearance of disjointed snippets of conversation scattered about the page. Your friend might have written one pithy comment two days ago, to which you replied, and another comment in response today. However, other activities are listed between the conversation comments. This can be a bit confusing as you're trying to read who said what. You can solve this dilemma by activating the Wall-to-Wall feature. Click the **See Wall-to-Wall** link below the comment to open another page in which the entire ongoing conversation appears without interruption.

Friends who also view your profile page can use the same tool to read the conversation.

Customizing Your Mini-Feed

You can customize how your stories appear on the Wall. You can click the **Settings** link in the upper-right corner of the Wall page to view settings you can turn on or off. If you don't see the link, click the **Options** link and the link changes to **Settings**. When the link is activated, a page similar to Figure 6.6 appears. You can control how imported stories are posted, whether comments are expanded, or even whether you allow postings from others. Simply make your selections; then click the first filter link to return to your regular Wall view. Any changes you made are now reflected on the Wall.

FIGURE 6.6   You can customize your Wall stories using these settings.

> **Tip**
>
> Speaking of customizing, you can also customize your Wall using other applications, such as Pieces of Flair, Super Wall, and Graffiti. These applications can help you jazz up your Wall a bit. Although you can't go as crazy with customizing as you can on MySpace, Facebook applications can help you bring a little flair to your pages. Learn more about Facebook applications in Lesson 12, "Adding Applications."

Tracking News Feeds

Whenever you want to see what everyone else is up to, click the **Home** link on the navigation bar (the blue bar at the top of any Facebook page). The Home page, shown in Figure 6.7, displays the constantly updating stories, or *live stream*, that comprise the news feed about your friends and what they're up to on Facebook. You can read through the list and find out what's happening, view thumbnails of photos, and find out what silly quizzes they're taking or what applications they're using.

FIGURE 6.7 The Home page displays the news feed.

You can filter your news feed display using the filters on the left. For example, to view only the status updates of your friends, click **Status Updates**. To view only new photo postings, click **Photos**. To return to the regular news feed again, click the **News Feed** filter. If you have more filters available, you can click the **More** link to view them. You can use the **Create** link to create a friends list (see Lesson 3, "Connecting with Friends," to learn more).

You can choose to hide the stories from people you don't want to see. Move your mouse pointer over the story and look for a **Hide** button that appears in the upper-right corner of the story. Click it, and Facebook hides all the stories in the news feed from that particular person. To add them back in again, scroll to the bottom of the Home page and click the **Edit Options** link. This opens a dialog box that keeps track of people you've "hidden" from view. You can add a person back in again at any time.

You can also hide postings from applications in the same way. Just click the **Hide** button, then click the application name.

Here are a few more things you can do with the news feed:

- ▶ You can click a person's name in your news feed to immediately open the person's profile page.

- ▶ You can add to the person's story by clicking the **Comment** link and adding a comment.

- ▶ Rather than type up a comment, you can click the **Like** link in the story.

- ▶ You can click a photo to open the album and view a larger picture.

- ▶ You can click a link to view the associated web page.

- ▶ You can click a video to view a video clip.

- ▶ You can click a "take this quiz" or "vote on this poll" or similar link to participate in the same activity listed.

- ▶ You can click an application link to add the listed application for yourself.

▶ When you scroll to the bottom of the Home page, you can click the **Older Posts** link to view more stories.

Managing Notifications

As mentioned at the beginning of this lesson, notifications are messages from Facebook to alert you to stories or activities that involve you somehow. If a friend tags you in a note, for example, or joins your group, you'll see a notification. Some applications you use also generate notifications concerning you automatically. You can view a brief listing of notifications by clicking the **Notifications** icon on the Applications bar, as shown in Figure 6.8. The icon often has a red number that pops up next to it, indicating how many notifications you have waiting to be read.

FIGURE 6.8 Activate the Notifications icon to see a menu of recent notifications.

For a full-on display of all your notifications, however, you need to open the Notifications tab. Switch over to your Inbox page by clicking the **Inbox** link in the navigation bar; then click the **Notifications** tab (see Figure 6.9). This tab displays notifications sent from you or received from others. From here, you can view notifications and control which ones are active.

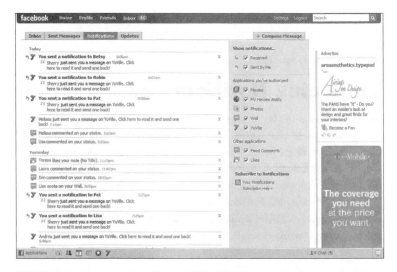

FIGURE 6.9   You can view all your notifications on the Notifications tab in your Inbox.

Tip
You can also make your way to the Notifications page by clicking the **Notifications** icon on the Applications bar (at the very bottom of the Facebook window) and then clicking **See All** on the menu.

Notifications are grouped chronologically by date, so today's notifications appear at the top of the page. Depending on the type of notification, you can click a link to read the message. You can use the check boxes on the right side of the page to control which notifications you see. For example, if you'd rather not see feed comments from applications, uncheck its check box. As you'll quickly learn, the more applications you add to your Facebook experience, the more notifications you'll see. You can easily stop pesky notifications from annoying applications by turning them off. Simply deselect the individual application's check box on the Notifications page.

Note

It's easy to confuse notifications with requests, and with some appli-cations, the information may appear in both formats. Notifications focus on notifying you, like a mini-news bulletin. Requests focus on inviting you to action, such as befriending someone or joining a group. Just remember, requests appear at the top of the Home page over in the right corner. Notifications appear in a shortened menu list when you click the **Notifications** icon on the Applications bar, or you can see them all on the Notifications page.

Tip

You can subscribe to your notifications on Facebook, turning them into an RSS feed (which stands for Really Simple Syndication, for-mats for web feeds of updated content) that you can read through an RSS reader (like Google Reader or Bloglines). Just click the **Your Notifications** link just below the notification settings and follow the instructions.

Summary

In this lesson, you learned how to inform and stay informed on Facebook. You learned the lingo for Facebook news feeds, mini-feeds, and notifica-tions. You also found out how to manage your Wall, write on your friends' Walls, remove postings, and view Wall-to-Wall conversations. You learned how to use the news feed stream on your Home page to view news about your friends. Finally, you learned how notifications work in Facebook and how to view them. In the next lesson, you learn more about communicat-ing through Facebook.

LESSON 7

Communicating Through Facebook

In this lesson, you learn how to use Facebook tools to communicate with your friends, coworkers, family, and so on. You'll learn how to send private messages using the Inbox, share links and actions, blog with the Notes feature, and chat live.

How to Communicate on Facebook

You can't have a social networking site without avenues to communicate, and Facebook has plenty. You've already learned how to express yourself on your profile page by writing on your Wall. This particular form of communication is generated by you for the purpose of letting people know what you're up to. When they pop by your profile page, they see your activities and any status updates you post to the Wall. You've also learned how to add a status update directly from the Home page so it appears out in the news feed for others to see on their Home pages, too.

Wall communication goes both ways—friends can write on your Wall, and you can also write on your friends' Walls to communicate with them. You might write a new posting, or comment on existing postings on a friend's Wall. Anyone else who views the friend's page can also see your postings and comments.

If you join a group, you can communicate through postings on the group Wall. You can learn more about Facebook groups in Lesson 10, "Joining Groups." Like any other Wall communication, when you share postings in a group, everyone in the group can see them.

Communicating with Wall postings can be a bit limiting at times. If you're looking to share a longer chunk of text than will fit in a status update, for example, you can use Facebook's Notes application. Notes are perfect for sharing larger amounts of text, and you can use the feature to communicate by blogging. With the Notes application, you can even include some basic HTML coding to enhance the note text.

If you're looking for more direct, less public ways to communicate, you can use the Facebook Inbox to send and receive messages. Just like any email client you use, the Inbox has options for reading messages, creating and sending messages, and organizing received messages. If you're looking for more immediate communication, try Facebook's live chat feature. You can talk with your friends (via your keyboard) who are logged on at the same time as you.

Finally, you can also communicate through sending Facebook actions and gifts. Sounds, weird, right? Don't knock it until you try it! The remaining sections in this lesson show you how to use many of the communication avenues mentioned here, including how to communicate with actions and gifts.

Sending and Receiving Messages

You can send and receive messages through the Facebook Inbox feature. It works just like an email client, letting you send personal messages to your Facebook friends. You don't have to know the person's email address to send him a message; you just need to know his name. You can also attach items to a message, such as a photo or link.

To view the Inbox, click the **Inbox** link at the top of any Facebook page in the blue navigation bar. You can also hover your mouse button over the link and click **View Message Inbox**. Figure 7.1 shows an example of a typical Inbox.

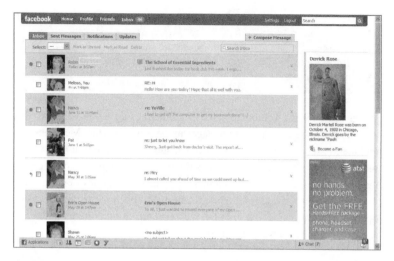

FIGURE 7.1   Use the Inbox to send personal messages to your Facebook friends.

The Inbox page features four tabs at the top of the page: Inbox, Sent Messages, Notifications, and Updates. Here's a rundown of what you can find on each tab:

Inbox   Use this tab to view your Inbox and the messages you've received.

Sent Messages   Click this tab when you want to view all the messages you've sent.

Notifications   This tab displays all your Facebook notifications—information about various activities that somehow involved you, such as being tagged in a photo or included in a comment string. (See Lesson 6, "Tracking Wall Postings, News Feeds, and Notifications," to learn more about using this tab.)

Updates   Use this tab to find updates on fan pages you subscribe to or support.

Tip
Facebook lets you know how many unread messages you have waiting in the Inbox by displaying the number next to the Inbox link on the navigation bar.

When you click the **Inbox** tab, a list of all the messages you've received appears, with the most recent messages at the top of the list. Messages include the sender's picture, if applicable, subject, and the first line of the message text. Facebook also includes the time and date of the message. To read a message, click it to open a message window, similar to Figure 7.2. You can click the message title or content line to open the message. Once opened, you can write a reply to the message, attach other items to the reply, and send it back to the person.

FIGURE 7.2   When you open a message to read it, a new window opens along with a Reply box you can use to send back a reply.

To reply to a message you've received, click in the **Reply** box in the message window and type out your reply; then click the **Send** button.

If you're messaging one person and keep replying to the original message, the message text accumulates like a thread on a news posting or discussion board. You can see the previous messages along with a Reply box for continuing the conversation.

Caution

Be careful about replying to group messages or messages that were addressed to multiple people. Because they were sent out to a group, the reply goes to the entire group as well. You'll notice with group messages that the Reply box becomes the Reply All box, and the **Send** button becomes the **Send to All** button. So don't accidentally type anything you don't want the whole group to know about. If you do want to reply to the sender only, look for the Reply link under his or her name on the message page.

Managing Messages

You can use the message indicator icons located on the far-left side of your messages to see the status of each message in your Inbox (see Figure 7.3). You can also click in the column where the indicators appear to make changes to the status of a message, such as marking a message as read or unread. One way to tell read messages from unread messages is by their background shading. Unread messages appear with a light, bluish shading as their background color. Read message have no shading.

Here's what each message indicator means:

▶ A blue dot to the left of a message means the message is unread. This mark disappears when you read the message.

▶ An arrow icon means you've replied to the message already.

▶ If a message includes an attachment, such as a photo, video, or link, a tiny graphical icon appears to indicate which type.

Here's how you can manage your messages:

▶ To mark it as unread again, move the mouse pointer to the left of the check box and click the dot that appears. You can also click the check box and then click the **Mark as Unread** link at the top of the Inbox to mark a message as unread.

▶ To mark a message as read again without opening the message, click the blue dot icon next to the message, or check the box and then click the **Mark as Read** link at the top of the Inbox.

FIGURE 7.3 Look to the message indicators to learn more about a message's status.

▶ You can delete messages you no longer want to keep. Select the message by clicking its check box (on the far-left side); then click the **Delete** link at the top of the Inbox.

▶ To mark multiple messages with a new status or for deletion, click the check box in front of each one; then click a link at the top of the Inbox.

▶ To select your messages from the Inbox for editing, such as deleting the messages, click the **Select** pop-up menu and choose whether to select **Read**, **Unread**, **All**, or **None**.

▶ To search through your messages, click inside the **Search Inbox** field in the top-right corner and type a word or phrase you want to search for; then press **Enter** or **Return**.

Tip

You can also mark a message as unread when you open the message in its own window and click the **Mark as Unread** link at the bottom. You'll also find a link there for deleting the message.

Sending a Message

You can send messages to other Facebook users, or to people you know outside of the Facebook environment as long as you know their email address. To send a message on Facebook, display the Inbox page and follow these steps:

1. Click **Compose Message**. (You can also hover your mouse pointer over the **Inbox** link on the navigation bar; then click **Compose New Message**.)

   Facebook opens the Compose Message window, as shown in Figure 7.4.

FIGURE 7.4   The Compose Message form.

2. On the Compose Message form, the **To** field is selected and ready to go. Type in the name, friend list (if you want to email a group of friends on Facebook), or email address. As you start typing, Facebook displays a list of possible matches to choose from; you can select a name from the list or keep typing.

   To remove a name that's added to the To field, just click its **X** button, or select the name and press **Delete**.

3. Click in the **Subject** field and title your message.

  4. Click in the **Message** box and type in your message text.

     Optionally, you can use the **Attach** links to attach a video, link, photo, and so on. You may also see icons for other applications you've installed that allow you to send items.

  5. When you're ready to send, click the **Send** button.

You can message more than one person—just add additional names to the To field. You can add up to 20 names per message.

Sharing Links

You can share web content you stumble across on the Internet with your friends on Facebook. For example, if you find a YouTube clip you want others to see, or if you read an interesting news article you want others to read, you can share a link to the material. When you add a link using Facebook's Links application, the link appears on your profile page and also on the news feed on the Home page.

To share a link on your profile page, click in your status update box (the box that says "What's on your mind?," also known as the Facebook Publisher). As soon as you do, Facebook displays some action icons you can add to the update, including one for links. Click the **Link** icon to expand the status update to include a field for adding a link, as shown in Figure 7.5.

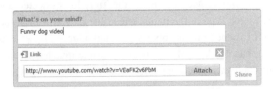

FIGURE 7.5 Use Facebook Publisher to add a comment and a link to your status update.

Facebook Publisher automatically adds the http:// prefix for you. Click in the field and type the URL to which you want to link. You can also paste a link you've copied from your browser window. Click the **Attach** button. Facebook may display a Security check box; type in the words that appear and click **Submit**. Finally, Facebook adds the link to the update. In Figure 7.6, a blog link is added. With photos and videos, you can choose which thumbnail image of the link to add. To add a comment to the link, just fill out the status update box. For example, you might write up an explanation of the link or why you're posting it. When you're ready to post the link, click the **Share** button.

FIGURE 7.6   You can control how the link appears in your news feed.

> **Tip**
> You can filter the news feed on your Home page to show only posted links by clicking the **Links** link located in the upper-left corner of the page.

If you want to link to a particular page on Facebook, such as an event, a group, or a note, you can quickly share it with others by clicking the **Share** button conveniently located on the page. When activated, this feature opens a Share box, similar to Figure 7.7, and you can choose to post the link publicly on your profile page or send it privately as a message to a friend.

> **Tip**
> You can bookmark a website in your browser and share the link on Facebook using the Share Bookmarklet tool. To do so, navigate to the Links page (click the **Applications** button in the bottom-left corner of the Facebook window and choose **Links**). Look for the **Share on Facebook** button, a gray button located on the right side of the page. You can drag it to your browser's Bookmarks bar. When you do, you can click it anytime you find a web page you want to share back on Facebook.

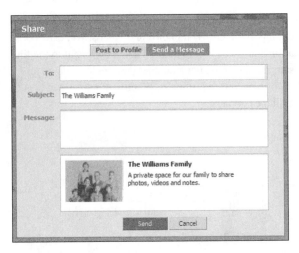

FIGURE 7.7   You can share a link to another Facebook page as a posted link on the news feed or as a message to a friend.

Sending Actions and Gifts

You can find lots of applications on Facebook that involve actions of some kind. The most famous is the default Poke application, probably because it has a tendency to be greatly overused by new members. A form of nonverbal communication, you can "poke" someone digitally as a way to say hi, much like a gentle punch to the shoulder or a nudge to the ribs, all without the need to type in any words. When you're viewing a friend's profile page, you can click the **Poke** link located underneath his or her profile picture (see Figure 7.8). If someone pokes you, Facebook lets you know with a notification. You can poke a person back, or ignore it.

There are hundreds of third-party applications that send other kinds of actions. For example, SuperPoke lets you send a kiss or a hug, cook a meal, karate chop, pinch, and so forth—all digitally imagined, of course. When you send someone an action from another application, they see a request and can respond by loading the application themselves and sending an action in return, or by ignoring your action entirely. For the office, you might try Office Poke, or for the romantically inclined, you might install Flirty Poke.

View Photos of Lisa (13)
Send Lisa a Message
Poke Lisa
Subscribe via SMS

FIGURE 7.8   Use the Poke feature to digitally poke a Facebook friend.

You can also send electronic gifts—and by electronic, I don't mean stereos and televisions, but rather digital artwork representing various items such as cupcakes, balloons, flowers, and so on. When you send a digital gift, a graphical icon of the gift appears on your friend's Gift Box area on his or her profile page. You might send a gift on a friend's birthday or anniversary, for example, or send a gift to cheer up someone.

There's a catch to gifting on Facebook, however. Gifts cost credits, which you must purchase online with a credit card. Most gifts cost about 10 credits, which is equivalent to a dollar. You can buy more credits, if needed, and purchase gifts whenever you want to send someone something special.

The Gifts application is a default part of Facebook. You can access it through the Applications menu at the bottom of the browser window. Just click the **Applications** link and then click **Gifts**. The Gifts page opens, as shown in Figure 7.9, and you can choose and pay for a gift (or gifts) to send.

You can learn more about adding other applications to your Facebook experience in Lesson 12, "Adding Applications."

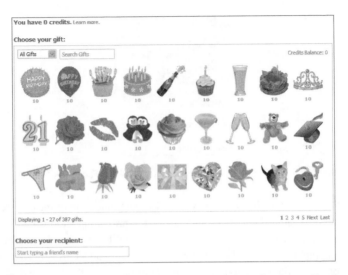

FIGURE 7.9   Use the Gifts application to send digital gifts to your Facebook friends.

Blogging with Notes

The Notes feature is another of Facebook's default applications. You can use Notes to share longer chunks of text than will fit in the typical status update box. You can even add photos to your notes. Notes are perfect for blogging on Facebook and sharing the blog with your friends. When you post a note, it appears on your profile page and in the news feed. You do have the choice of setting a privacy level for the note. You can choose for everyone to see it, people on your networks and friends lists, friends of friends, only friends, or customize and only allow select friends to see the note. After a note is published, others can add their comments to the note.

To use the Notes tool, follow these steps:

1. Click the + tab on your profile page and then click **Notes**.

   The Notes page tab is added to your profile page.

   First add the Notes application to your profile page tabs.

2. Click the **Write a New Note** button.

Facebook displays the Write a Note page with a blank note form, as shown in Figure 7.10.

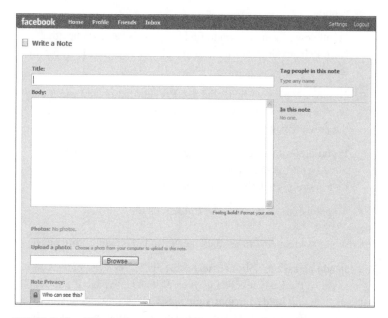

FIGURE 7.10   Fill out the note form to create your note or blog.

3. Click in the **Title** box and type in a title for your note.

4. Click in the **Body** box and type in your note text.

> **Tip**
>
> You can easily copy and paste text from another program into your Facebook Notes feature. For example, you might compose your blog in Microsoft Word and copy the text into the Facebook form.

Optionally, you can tag Facebook friends you mention in your note using the **Tag people in this note** field. This lets them know with a notification that they're somehow involved in your note.

Optionally, you can click the **Browse** button to add a photo to the note, or add one from an existing Facebook photo album. When you add a photo, additional options appear for controlling the photo's position on the note page, and a box for adding a caption.

5. Scroll down the note form to find the privacy setting; click the **Note Privacy** drop-down menu and choose a privacy level for the note.

6. To preview the note first, click the **Preview** button and check out how your note will look on Facebook. You can publish it from the preview page, or click **Edit** to return to the Notes page.

   If you prefer to save the draft and open it again later, click the **Save Draft** button. To change your mind about the whole note idea entirely, click the **Discard** button.

7. To publish the note, click the **Publish** button.

To view your note at any time, click the **Notes** tab on your profile page.

You can add pizzazz to your note text using HTML coding. In the bottom-right corner of the Body text box of your Write a Note page is a little link that says "**Feeling bold? Format your note.**" Click this link to view a listing of HTML tags you can type in to add formatting to your text. If you already know HTML coding, you can type it straight in as you compose your note. If you don't, you can use the handy cheat sheet offered by Facebook; print it out and have it handy.

You can click the **Applications** button at the bottom of the browser window and then click **Notes** to open the Facebook Notes page, which displays your friends' notes as well as your own. You can also filter your news feed on the Home page to show your friends' recent notes, including your own. Just click the **Notes** link.

Chatting with Friends

If messages, notes, and digital pokes aren't enough ways to communicate on Facebook, you can also talk directly to friends using the Chat tool. If a friend is logged on the same time as you, you can have real-time conversations. If you've chatted with other Chat programs, like Yahoo! Messenger, you'll find that the Facebook Chat tool works the same way.

The first thing to do is switch your online status. Click the **Chat** icon on the far-right side of the Application bar at the bottom of the browser window. The Chat menu appears, as shown in Figure 7.11. Click the **Options** button and click **Go Offline**. This command can be toggled on or off. When it's on, there's a green dot next the Chat icon. If it's off, the dot changes to gray. After your status is green, you're good to go.

FIGURE 7.11   Turn your Chat status to online.

Now you have to find someone to chat with; click the **Chat** icon again to see a list of your Facebook friends who are currently online. If they're available for a chat, you'll see them listed in the Chat menu when you click the Chat icon. To start chatting, click the friend's name in the list. Facebook opens a mini chat window, similar to Figure 7.12. Type in what you want to say in the field at the bottom of the chat window, and press **Enter** or **Return**. The text appears in the conversational area of the window, and continues to scroll by as you keep chatting. You can use the scroll bar to revisit parts of the conversation. You can chat with multiple users, but not multiple conversations with many users in one chat window.

To close the window and stop chatting, just click the window's **Close** button (X) in the upper-right corner. You can also minimize the window to move it out of the way. If the window is minimized, Facebook displays a red balloon icon to let you know the other person has typed in more conversation.

FIGURE 7.12 You can type in the bottom area of the chat window to start chatting.

To create a larger chat window, click the main **Chat** icon again and click the **Options** button. Next, click the **Pop out Chat** command. Facebook displays a large chat window you can view more easily. Repeat the steps to return the window to a mini-window size again.

When you click the **Options** button in the main Chat menu, you can see additional chat options to choose from, as follows:

Show Feed stories in Chat   Displays any stories, such as status updates or shared links, about you or your friend to appear in the chat window.

Play Sound for New Messages   Sounds an alert noise when a new conversation line is added to the chat window.

Keep Online Friends Window Open   Keeps the Chat menu listing of online friends open at all times, until minimized by you.

Show Only Names in Online Friends   Hides the profile pictures in the Chat menu to save some space.

Friend Lists   Lets you display a Friends list and display the lists in Chat.

Summary

In this lesson, you learned how to communicate with friends on Facebook using messages, silly actions, blogging, sharing links, and chatting. In the next lesson, you'll learn how to share photos and videos.

LESSON 8

Sharing Photos

In this lesson, you learn how to view and add photos in Facebook. You'll learn how to create an album, upload pictures, and publish the whole thing on Facebook. You'll also learn how to tag people in your photos and organize your photos within Facebook.

Sharing Photos on Facebook

Would you believe that Facebook is the largest photo-sharing site on the Web? It's true. It surpasses popular sites like Photobucket and Flickr, among others. Facebook users upload millions of photos each month. Why? Because it's easy, a fun way to share stuff about yourself, a perfect way to connect with others, and a great marketing tool, just to list a few reasons. It might also help that Facebook lets you post gobs of photos. As of 2009, users have uploaded over 10 billion photos on the social net-working site. That's a lot of pictures.

Photos you add to Facebook are organized into photo *albums*, just like you'd do with actual photographs at home. An album can hold one photo or up to 200. You can also create as many albums as you like. You might make an album of vacation pictures, artistic images, snapshots of your friends and family, and so on. When you post photos, you can add cap-tions and tag people in the photos, and other users can add comments to your photos.

All your photo activities on Facebook are handled through a built-in application called, appropriately, Photos. The application, which is part of the default apps available when you start your Facebook account, offers tools for uploading photos, organizing photos, and sharing photos. You can utilize three different uploaders, applications to help you move your photos from your computer or camera onto Facebook, one of which is made for Mac users.

You can share photos on your profile page, in the news feed out on the Home page, in messages and notes, in group postings, and more. One of the easiest ways to view your friends' photos is when you see them posted as a story on the news feed on your Home page, as shown in Figure 8.1. Just click a photo to open the image in its own window, or click the album name located below the photo to open the associated album.

FIGURE 8.1   Posted photos often appear as stories on the news feed on your Home page.

Tip

You can also look for links to photo albums over in the Highlights area of your Home page. Located below the Requests notifications area on the far-right side of the page, just below the sponsored advertisement, the Highlights area lists some popular activities, causes, and events your friends are attending, sponsoring, or visiting. It also lists recently posted albums.

Another way to view photos is on profile pages. For example, if you're viewing your friend's profile page, you can click a photo in her mini-feed stories, or you can click her **Photos** tab and view her listed albums. Figure 8.2 shows an example of photos posted on the mini-feed of a profile page.

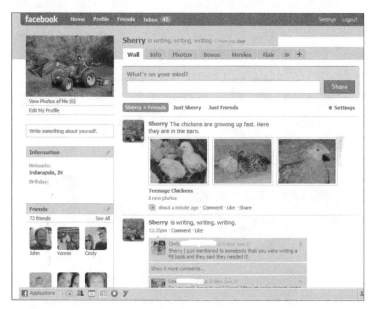

FIGURE 8.2   Another way to view photos is on profile pages.

If you're looking for an all-encompassing spot to view photos, visit the Photos application page. The next section tells you how.

Viewing the Photos Application Page

To find your way to the Photos application, you can click the **Applications** button on the Applications bar, located at the bottom of the browser window in the far-left corner. When clicked, the **Applications** menu appears, and you can then select **Photos**. This opens the Photos page, as shown in Figure 8.3. You can also click the **Photos** icon, also conveniently located on the Applications bar (looks like a stack of photos), to open the Photos application page.

FIGURE 8.3   Use the Photos page to view your friends' photo albums.

The page features the following three tabs:

> **Recent Albums**   Displays recently posted albums from your friends.
>
> **Mobile Uploads**   Displays photos uploaded from mobile devices (cell phones).
>
> **Tagged Friends**   Displays photos of your friends who have been tagged in various albums.

You can peruse various albums and images among the three tabs. To view an album, just click the album cover. Your friend's album opens to show the photos it contains, as shown in Figure 8.4.

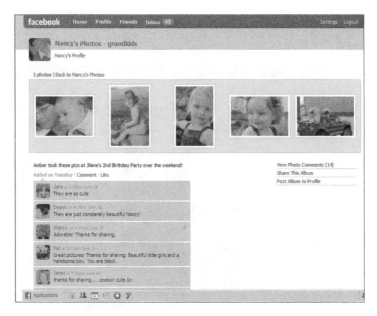

FIGURE 8.4   You can click an image to view the photo, or add comments out on the album page.

To start viewing each photo individually, just click a photo and Facebook opens it as its own page, similar to Figure 8.5. You can click the **Previous** and **Next** buttons at the top-right corner of the photo to move back and forth through the album's pictures like a slide show. You can also navigate back to the album or the profile page using the links on the top left.

At the bottom of the album page and the bottom of each picture page, there's a place where you and your friends can add comments. This feature is a great way to converse about the picture, the subject, or the experience it represents. It's not uncommon to see entire conversations unfold in the comment section of a photo or album cover.

The page includes options for sharing the photo with others, tagging someone in the photo, or reporting any photo that violates the Facebook terms of service. Not that you need to be reminded, but there are some restrictions in what types of photos you can share on Facebook. So if you're hoping to start your own online pornography magazine, Facebook is not the way to go. You can check out Facebook's Terms of Service page to learn more about rules and conduct on the site. See Lesson 4, "Finding Help with Facebook Services and Etiquette," to find out more.

FIGURE 8.5   You can view photos individually in their own window, and progress through each image like a slide show.

To share a photo or album with another friend, you can click the **Share** button or **Share this Album** link to open the Share dialog box. From there, you can share the album by posting a link on your news feed, or by emailing a link to a friend.

Tip

Tagging is when you identify someone in the photo, and Facebook sends out a notification to the person and mentions it in their mini-feed. Learn more about tagging later in this lesson.

Adding Your Own Photos

Now that you know a little about how to view photos in Facebook, it's time to add some of your own. First you need to locate and decide which photos you want to share online. After you've figured that out, you're ready to create an album and upload some photos.

The process of adding photos occurs in three phases. The first phase is to establish an album to hold the photos on Facebook. The second phase is to use the Photo Uploader to actually select and upload the photo files. The third phase is to publish the photos.

Creating an Album

You can easily create a new photo album from your profile page. You can also control who has access to your photos using the Privacy controls. The default privacy setting is **Everyone**; however, you might want to narrow this down to just friends, or you can customize it to include only certain friends or networks.

Follow these steps to start an album:

1. From your profile page, click the **Photos** tab to open your Photos and the Photos application.

> **Note**
>
> If this is your first time using the Photos app, you may have to add it's tab to your profile page. Click the **Add a new Tab** button (the giant plus sign), then click **Photos**. Now you're ready to go.

2. Click the **Create a Photo Album** button.

The Add New Photos page appears, as shown in Figure 8.6.

3. Click in the **Album Name** text box in the Create Album tab and type a name for the album.

4. Optionally, in the **Location** box, type in the location in which the pictures were taken.

FIGURE 8.6   Fill out the album form.

5. Click in the **Description** box and type up a description of the album, such as what it's about, and so on.

6. Click the **Privacy** drop-down arrow and select a privacy setting for the album. The setting is Everyone, unless you choose differently.

7. Click **Create Album**.

    Facebook opens the Upload Photos page (see Figure 8.7). Continue to the next section to learn how to select and upload photos.

Tip

When you activate the **Customize** option in the **Privacy** drop-down menu, a separate dialog box form opens, and you can specify who you want to allow and even who you do not want to allow access to your photos. You can specify certain people by name, and you can choose to allow an entire network.

Note

Back in Lesson 2, "Setting Up a Profile," you learned how to add a profile picture. The same techniques are used to add other photos. You can add more profile pictures whenever you like. All your profile pictures are organized in a default album called, appropriately, "Profile Pictures." To view this album, just look for it among the other albums on your Photos tab. You can edit existing photos, add new ones, and remove ones you no longer want.

Uploading Photos

You can choose from three different uploaders to help you move pictures from your computer or camera onto Facebook. You can use the Java-based Photo Uploader, the Simple Uploader, or if you're a Mac user, you can install and use the iPhoto Exporter. The iPhoto Exporter is used within your iPhoto program. Regardless of your uploader choice, the Upload Photos page is where it all happens.

Note

You'll need a newer version of the Java plug-in on your Web browser to use Facebook's uploader, at least version 1.6.0_07.

The Upload Photos page, shown in Figure 8.7, is the place to select and upload your digital photos. You may have to grant the application authorization to use it, especially if this is the first time you're using it. The Photo Uploader is a Java-based program, so you might also have to okay it with your browser program. If you prefer not to use a Java-based application, you can use the Simple Uploader application instead. You might also be asked during the process to verify that the photos are yours and distributable by you. That's all part of Facebook's quest to keep the site legal and on the up-and-up.

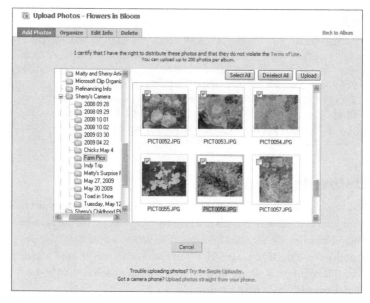

FIGURE 8.7   Use Facebook's Photo Uploader to choose your photos and upload them onto the site.

Follow these steps to upload photos using the Java-based Photo Uploader:

1. From the Upload Photos page, use the left pane to navigate to the folder containing the pictures you want to upload.

2. In the right pane, select the photo or photos you want to add to the album by clicking to add a check mark in the photo's check box. You can use the scroll bars to move through the list. To select all the photos, click the **Select All** button.

3. When you're ready to upload, click the **Upload** button at the top of the Uploader page.

   The photos are uploaded and a box appears so you can monitor their uploading status. Depending on how many photos you chose and your connection speed, the process may take a few seconds or a few minutes.

4. When the upload is complete, click **OK**.

To use another uploader instead of the Java-based one explained here, skip ahead to the section "Using Other Photo Uploaders" to learn more.

Publishing Your Photos

After you upload photos (regardless of which uploader you use), Facebook displays the Edit Album page, as shown in Figure 8.8. You can use this page to add captions to your photos, choose an album cover, or organize the photos into other albums. The album cover is just the photo that appears in the listing of albums and when the story is posted on your profile or news feed. By default, the Photos application makes the first photo the album cover, but you can choose any photo in the album as the cover.

You have several options to choose from on the Edit Album page:

▶ To publish the photos as is, without any changes, just click the **Publish Now** button.

▶ To add a caption, just click in the **Caption** box in front of each photo and type one up.

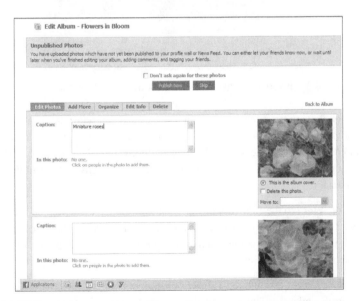

FIGURE 8.8   The Edit Album page lets you add captions and publish your photos.

- ▶ To make a photo the album cover, click the **This is the album cover** radio button.

- ▶ To remove a photo you decide you don't want to include, click the **Delete this photo** check box.

- ▶ To relocate the photo to another existing album, click the **Move to** drop-down arrow and choose an album from the list.

- ▶ To forgo publishing the photos right now, click the **Skip** button at the top of the page.

- ▶ To save all the changes you make to the Edit Album page, click the **Save Changes** button located at the very bottom of the page.

When you are presented with the Unpublished Photos prompt, as shown in Figure 8.9, click **Publish** to publish the photos to your profile and the news feed on the Home page. To skip the publishing process for now, click the **Skip** button, and you can choose to publish the photos later.

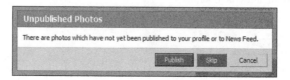

FIGURE 8.9   If you're ready to publish, click the Publish button.

If you do skip the publishing action for now, you can return to the album, and publish the photos any time. To do so, open the album in your **Photos** tab of the profile page and click the **Edit Photos** link. This opens the Edit Album page again, and you can finish any edits and activate the **Publish** command.

If you return to the Edit Album page, you can use the other tabs on the page to add more photos to the album, change the order of the photos, edit the album information (such as title, location, and description), or delete the album entirely.

As you browse through individual photos in your album, you can also find controls under the photo for rotating the image. Look for the icons with a clockwise arrow and counterclockwise arrow; click to rotate one way or the other.

> **Note**
>
> You can invite people outside the Facebook website to view your albums using the public link Facebook provides. Open the album to the Edit Album page and scroll to the bottom to find a unique URL you can copy and paste into an email message. The recipient can then follow the link and view your images. Of course, it would be cooler if they'd just join in the fun and make a Facebook account.

Using Other Photo Uploaders

If you prefer not to use Facebook's Java-based uploader, you can use the Simple Uploader. There's a link for it on the Upload Photos page. Click the **Try the Simple Uploader** link to open the page shown in Figure 8.10. Next, click the **Browse** button and navigate to the photo file you want to open and select it. The Simple Uploader adds it to the first field. You can continue adding more photos, as needed—up to five at a time. If you need to add more, you'll have to do so in batches of five. Be sure to check the certification check box to tell Facebook the photos are yours and distributable by you. When you're ready to upload the images, click the **Upload Photos** button.

FIGURE 8.10   You can also use the Simple Uploader to upload photos.

The rest of the process is the same as using the Java-based Photo Uploader covered in the previous sections.

If you're a Mac user, you can add the iPhoto Exporter application to your computer and use it to upload photos from the iPhoto application directly. Look for a link at the bottom of the Upload Photos page that says "**Use iPhoto on your Mac? Check out the Facebook Exporter for iPhoto**." Click it and download the Facebook Exporter for iPhoto application. You can then install the application and use iPhoto to upload photos into a Facebook album.

iPhoto Exporter simply adds a Facebook tab to the Export Photos dialog box, as shown in Figure 8.11, where you can create a new album for Facebook or insert the photos in an existing album. You can also use the dialog box to add captions and tags before uploading the images. To navigate to the dialog box and see for yourself, open iPhoto and select the files you want to import. Next, click the **File** menu and then click **Export**. When the Export Photos dialog box opens, you'll have to login to your Facebook account to start the process. After your browser logs you in, you're returned to the Export Photos dialog box, where you can continue the process of uploading the files. Just click the **Export** button and follow the prompts. When the import is complete, you can review the album on Facebook and approve the uploaded images. After you've approved the images, you can post the album to your profile, and you're done. .

If you have photos on a camera phone, you can upload them to Facebook as well. Look for a link at the bottom of the Upload Photos page that says "**Got a camera phone? Upload photos straight from your phone**." When you click this link, the Facebook Mobile page opens, and you can upload your photos using an MMS. Learn more about Facebook's mobile features in Lesson 15, "Making Facebook Mobile." .

FIGURE 8.11   Mac users can add a Facebook tab to iPhoto's Export Photos dialog box for uploading image files.

Tagging People in Photos

Tagging is a popular activity on Facebook. Tagging is when you identify someone in a story, photo, or video. When you tag someone, Facebook lets them know with a notification so they can go take a look at the story. The tag also appears as a story in their mini-feed on their profile page. In the case of photos, you can tag people to identify them in the picture. You can even tag people in a photo who aren't on Facebook and send them an email.

To tag a person in a picture, follow these steps:

1. Open the photo you want to tag.

2. Scroll below the photo and click the **Tag This Photo** link.

3. The mouse pointer turns into a cross-hair pointer when you move it over the photo. Click the person you want to identify in the photo to open a tag box, as shown in Figure 8.12.

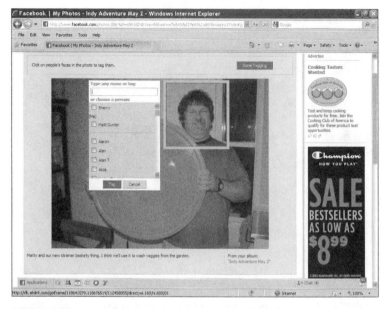

FIGURE 8.12 You can tag people in a photo to identify them.

4. Click a name from the list or type in the person's name.

If you type someone's name who isn't in your Friends list, you have the option of emailing the person a link to the image.

5. Click the **Tag** button, and the person is tagged.

6. Click the **Done Tagging** button above the photo when you finish tagging everyone in the photo.

When you add a tag, anyone viewing the photo can move their mouse over the people in the photo and view the tag that points out who each person is. Very handy, don't you think?

To de-tag a person, you can reopen the photo and click the **remove tag** that appears beneath the photo under the caption text. People you've tagged can also remove their tags from your photos using the same step.

You can also tag yourself in someone else's photos, but they'll have to approve of the tag before everyone else can see it.

Organizing and Editing Your Photos

It's easy to organize and edit your photos after you have created an album. For example, you may decide you need to reorder the photos, or add captions. Or you may want to delete a photo, or completely remove an entire album.

One way to revisit an album and make changes is to click the **Photos** tab on your profile page. Locate the album you want to work with and click the album name or cover image to open the album. Facebook opens a page similar to Figure 8.13. The links at the top of the photos take you to various tabs on the Edit Album page to make changes. Always click the **Save Changes** button at the bottom of the page you edit to keep any changes you make. Because the button is often hidden from view, it's easy to overlook its existence.

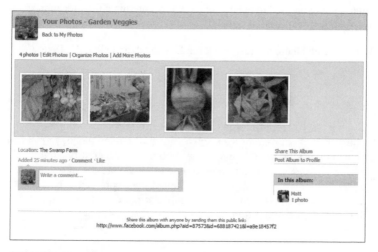

FIGURE 8.13 Open an album to find links for editing, organizing, and adding more photos.

If you click the **Edit Photos** link on the album's page, the Edit Album page opens with the Edit Photos tab displayed. You've seen this tab before back when you uploaded the photos just before publishing them. You can use this tab to add or edit captions, delete a photo, move a photo to another album, or designate a new album cover. Be sure to click the **Save Changes** button at the bottom of the page to keep any of the changes you make.

If you click the **Organize Photos** link on the album's page, the Edit Album page opens to the Organize tab and you can rearrange the order in which the photos appear. Just drag a photo and drop it where you want it to appear. Don't forget to click the **Save Changes** button to save the new arrangement.

If you click the **Add More Photos** link on the album's page, the Add More tab opens, and you can use the same Photo Uploader (or another uploader) to add more photos to the album. This is the same page you used to upload the photos the first time around.

To edit the album information, such as the album name, location, or description, click the **Edit Info** tab and make your changes. This is the same screen you used to create the album by entering a title, location, description, and privacy level. .

To remove an album entirely, click the **Delete** tab and click the **Delete** button.

Note

The photos you remove aren't really gone. They still exist somewhere in Facebook's storage servers. For that reason alone, you should always be careful about what photos you do post online, avoiding photos that embarrass, or ones that violate the site's terms of service. You may think someone cannot find them again, but they're still out there somewhere. It's better not even to post questionable photos in the first place. When in doubt, opt out!

Summary

In this lesson, you learned how to upload and publish photos to share on Facebook. You learned how to tag people in a photo, use various uploader applications, and edit albums. In the next lesson, you learn how to share videos.

LESSON 9

Sharing Videos

In this lesson, you learn how to share your own original video clips on Facebook. You'll learn how to upload videos, play videos, record videos, and edit video information.

Sharing Videos on Facebook

You're not just limited to static images (that is, photos) on Facebook. You can also share videos. Whether you call them movies, videos, or multimedia clips, the result is still the same—a dynamic clip that you can play and watch. You can add videos to your profile page that, in turn, appear on the news feed of the Home page. You can also add videos to your notes and group pages, and even embed them on outside sites. Like photos, you can tag people in your videos, and add comments to them.

There are a few stipulations with using videos on Facebook, as follows:

- ▶ The video must be made by you or your friends.

- ▶ The video must be under 1024 MB in size and less than 20 minutes in length. If you're a brand new user, the limits may be smaller for you until you verify your account.

- ▶ The video should contain you or a friend.

Basically, you're not allowed to upload illegal copies of television shows, music videos, movies, or any content that's not made by you or a friend. The video content should be yours and yours alone. You're also expected to comply with Facebook's terms of service regarding the content you post. In other words, don't post copyrighted or pirated videos, or clips of questionable taste or subject matter. Facebook even makes you agree to this the first time you upload a video.

You can upload video clips you've previously recorded, such as videos from your camera or mobile device, or you can hook up your camera directly and record a new video. If your computer has a built-in camera and microphone, you can record directly from there. You can use Facebook's Video application to do all of these options.

Tip

To find out more about what's in Facebook's terms of service, you can click the **Terms** link at the very bottom of any Facebook page. To learn more, see Lesson 4, "Finding Help with Facebook Services and Etiquette."

Adding a Video

Adding a video is as easy as adding photos. You can use the Video tab on your profile page as one way to access the built-in Video application. The first time you display the tab, it's very blank. There are no videos to display, just two buttons: Upload and Record (see Figure 9.1).

To add a previously recorded video to Facebook, follow these steps:

1. From your profile page, click the **Video** tab.

If your Video tab isn't added yet, click the plus sign (+) and click **Video** from the menu that appears.

If your Video tab is added but hidden, click the double-arrow icon and click **Video**.

If this is your first time using Facebook's Video features, your page appears mostly blank, with just an **Upload** and **Record** button in the corner, as shown in Figure 9.1.

FIGURE 9.1   The video upload process works similarly to the photo upload process.

2. Click the **Upload** button.

The Create a New Video page appears, as shown in Figure 9.2.

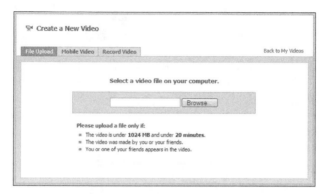

FIGURE 9.2 The first phase of uploading a video is locating it on your computer.

3. In the File Upload tab, click the **Browse** button; then navigate to and select the video file you want to upload.

4. If this is your first time uploading a video, Facebook displays an authorization box detailing the terms surrounding video usage on Facebook. Click **Agree**.

Facebook displays an information form, as shown in Figure 9.3, and the uploading process begins. Depending on your connection speed and file size, the process may take a few minutes. While waiting for the upload to finish, you can fill out the rest of the form.

5. Click in the **Title** box and type a title for the video.

6. Click in the **Description** box and type a description for the video.

7. Click the **Privacy** drop-down menu and specify a privacy level.

8. When the upload is complete or while it's finishing, click the **Save Info** button.

The video now appears on your Video page, as shown in Figure 9.4, as well as on your profile page and in the news feed on the Home page. To play the clip, click the **Play** button.

FIGURE 9.3 Fill out a title and description for the clip and set a privacy level.

FIGURE 9.4 The new video appears on your Video page.

Learn how to record a new video later in this lesson.

Viewing Videos

To view videos posted by others, you can click the **Video** link on the Home page to filter the news feed to show all the video clips your friends have posted. You can also play a video clip directly in the news feed by clicking its **Play** button, as shown in Figure 9.5. This enables you to view the clip without opening it in its own window.

If you move your mouse pointer over the bottom of the video image while the clip is playing, a bar of player controls appears (see Figure 9.6). The player has controls for pausing the clip, muting the clip, or showing it full-screen size. The controls only appear when the clip is playing.

FIGURE 9.5   You can play videos directly in the news feed on the Home page by clicking the Play button on the video's thumbnail image.

Here's how to use the player controls:

- ▶ Click the **Pause** button to stop the clip. When the pause action is in effect, the **Play** button appears in its place to start the clip again.

- ▶ To mute the clip, click the **Speaker** icon.

- ▶ To adjust the sound, drag the audio level up or down.

FIGURE 9.6 You can move your mouse over the bottom of a clip to view player controls.

> ▶ To view the clip in a full-size window, click the **Window** icon on the far-right end of the player controls.

If you do want to play a video in the news feed in its own window, click the video title link beneath the thumbnail image.

If you're viewing a friend's profile page and she has a video clip, you can click the **Play** button to view the clip in her mini-feed. To share the video clip with someone else, click the **Share** link to open the Share box. You can choose to post the clip to your own profile page for sharing, or send it as a message. You can find this same **Share** link on the news feed on the Home page, too.

You and your friends can add comments to your video clip in the same way they add comments to photos, using a Comment box. You can add comments directly to a clip on the news feed by clicking the **Comment** link to open a Comment box and typing in your text. You can also add a comment to a video from its video window by clicking in the **Comment** box below the video image and typing in your text.

To find your way back to your own videos, open your profile page and click the **Video** tab. The tab lists all the videos you've posted. To play one, click the video to open it in its own window and click the **Play** button.

Editing Your Videos

To edit a video and change the description or title, or tag the subjects, display your **Video** tab on your profile page, as shown in Figure 9.7. Remember, only so many tabs show up on your profile page, so if you don't see it listed, click the double-arrow tab and then click **Video**.

FIGURE 9.7   Your Video tab shows all your uploaded videos.

Next, click the video you want to edit from the list to open the Your Videos page, as shown in Figure 9.8.

From here, you can do the following:

▶ Click the **Edit This Video** link below the video player and make changes to the information, such as give it a new title or description.

▶ Click the **Tag This Video** link to open a field below the player area and type in the name of the person you're tagging. Click the **Done Tagging** button when you finish.

▶ Click the **Delete Video** link to remove the video entirely. You'll have to confirm the removal by clicking the Delete button that appears when Facebook warns you that the deletion is permanent.

▶ You can use the rotation icons to rotate the video clockwise or counterclockwise, if needed.

▶ Click the **Embed this Video** link to open an Embed Your Video box containing the coding needed to embed the video on any web page. Just copy and paste the coding.

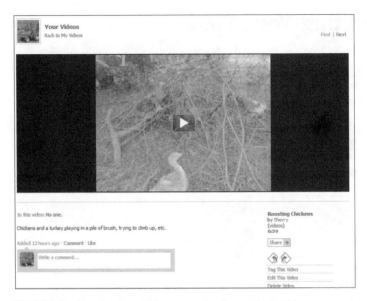

Your Videos
Back to My Videos

First | Next

In this video: No one.

Chickens and a turkey playing in a pile of brush, trying to climb up, etc.

Added 13 hours ago · Comment · Like

Write a comment...

Roosting Chickens
by Sheery
(videos)
0:59

Share +

Tag This Video
Edit This Video
Delete Video

FIGURE 9.8   Use the Your Videos page to view a single video.

Recording a New Video

If your computer has a built-in camera and microphone, or if you have a digital video recorder you can hook up to your computer, you can record your own video clips to post on Facebook. With a little help from Adobe's Flash Player, you can record and place the clips directly into Facebook, where they can be viewed on your profile page as well as the news feed out on the Home page.

Follow these steps to record a new video:

1. Open the Video tab on your profile page and click the **Record** button.

2. Facebook displays the Create a New Video page, as shown in Figure 9.9, and a Flash Player Settings dialog box in the middle requesting to allow Facebook access to your camera. Depending on the box you see, click the **Allow** radio button or the **Allow** check box.

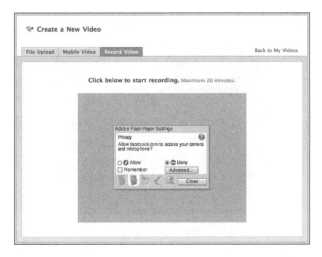

FIGURE 9.9 Before you start recording, you must allow Facebook access to your camera.

3. Depending on your prompt box, you may need to close it to continue; click **Close**.

4. When you're ready to start recording, click the **Record** button, as shown in Figure 9.10.

FIGURE 9.10 Click Record and yell "action," and the movie is rolling, so to speak.

5. Click the **Stop** button to stop recording (see Figure 9.11).

FIGURE 9.11 Click the Stop button to stop at any time.

Facebook displays more video controls, as shown in Figure 9.12.

FIGURE 9.12 When you stop recording, more video controls appear on the page, allowing you to reset and start over again, or to save what you've recorded.

If the recording did not go well, you can click the **Reset** button and try again.

6. If you're finished recording, click the **Save** button.

Facebook displays a form for filling out details about the video recording, as shown in Figure 9.13.

FIGURE 9.13 Fill out details about your video recording using the form.

7. If applicable, enter any friends (or yourself) to tag people in the video using the **In this video** box.

8. Type a name for the video in the **Title** box.

9. Type a description of the video in the **Description** box.

Optionally, you can choose a different thumbnail image for the video's "cover" to represent the video.

10. Click the **Privacy** drop-down arrow and choose a privacy setting for the video.

11. Click the **Save** button, and Facebook saves the recording and adds it to your video list.

You can return to the Video tab on your profile page to view the recording.

Summary

In this lesson, you learned how to share your video clips on Facebook. You learned how to upload existing clips, record new clips, and view clips found all over Facebook. In the next lesson, you'll learn how to join Facebook groups.

LESSON 10

Joining Groups

In this lesson, you learn how to find and join Facebook groups. You'll learn how to search for groups of interest, join a group, view group pages, and even create and manage your own group.

Socializing with Facebook Groups

Yet another way to socialize and network on Facebook is through groups. You can use Facebook groups to mix and mingle with people outside your friends list and make new friends along the way. Groups are gathering places generally organized around a common interest, such as a hobby, a favorite topic, or a cause. Groups run the gamut from silly to serious on Facebook, and it's not uncommon to find all kinds of humorous groups to join just for the fun of it, especially those attempting to break a record or participate in some type of social experiment. Need to agonize with someone over your ongoing shoe-shopping problem? There's a group for that. Do you want to commiserate with fellow foodies over the quest for a good steak? There's a group for that. Do you want to link up with fellow aircraft enthusiasts or civil war buffs? There are groups for that. The possibilities are endless and waiting for you to explore, and you'll quickly see that there are hundreds and hundreds of groups out there.

Groups are the perfect venue for sharing ideas, passions, social and political issues, or just creating a place to connect. Many groups offer discussion boards, as well as the all-purpose Wall for communicating. You can learn a lot from specialty subject groups, or find an avenue to post questions to others about a topic you want to know more about. Chances are, you'll find somebody willing to offer information in no time at all.

You can search for different kinds of groups, as well as create your own group. You're bound to find a group to suit your needs. For example, if you're into politics, you can find a group based around your political leanings, or if you're a reality TV show addict, you can find a group of fellow fans to share news. Many companies, politicians, celebrities, musicians, and even products have avid groups going on Facebook as well as on their Pages (learn the difference between groups and Pages in Lesson 13, "The Professional Side of Facebook: Pages). You can even find groups about Facebook itself. If you can't find a group for your topic of interest, you can create your own group and invite others to join.

Groups can attract hundreds or thousands of people, or just a few. Groups form to air grievances, express ideologies, or just gush about a favorite actor or band. Groups can also be a powerful tool to spread a message, organizing people into grassroots movements, social causes, and more. Election years create a lot of groups on Facebook, as you can imagine. Figure 10.1 shows an example of one of the more popular groups on the site, "People Who Always Have To Spell Their Names For Other People," a group that offers solace to people with unusually spelled names. As of this writing, the group has over 500,000 members and growing.

Groups are run by an administrator, usually the person who created the group. Larger groups may also include additional administrators to help manage the postings and moderate the discussions that take place in the group. Depending on the group and what's allowed, group members can share comments, participate in a discussion group, and post photos, videos, links, and so on.

Facebook groups are divided into three main types, as follows:

Open   Open groups allow anyone on Facebook to join. You can join yourself, or invite your friends.

Closed   Closed groups are more exclusive and require an invitation to join. You can also ask to join a closed group, and it's up to the administrator to let you in or not.

Secret   Secret groups are not advertised anywhere on Facebook, and can only be joined by invitation.

FIGURE 10.1   An example of a typical group page on Facebook.

Now that you know a little about groups, it's time to find groups and join up.

Caution

Watch out for spammers! It's not uncommon to find spamming going on among the Facebook groups, such as people selling products and services or get-rich schemes. Although spamming isn't allowed on Facebook, it still occurs. You can report a spam posting by clicking the **Report** link found next to or below the posting.

Finding a Group

One way to find a group is to pay attention to the news feed on the Home page to see what groups your friends are joining. If you see something interesting, give it a try. You might also spot an interesting group to join

while perusing your friends' profiles. For serious group exploration, however, you can conduct a search.

You can use the **Search** field at the top of any Facebook page to search
for a specific topic. You can also open the Groups application. The
Groups app, a default application that's part of the Facebook environment,
is the place to go to view your groups and friends' groups, and to search
for new groups. To navigate to the page, click the **Applications** button at
the bottom of the browser window and then click **Groups** or click the
Groups button, also located on the Applications bar.

The Groups page looks similar to Figure 10.2. The links at the top of the
page take you to a page of your groups, a search page to help you find
more groups, and a page of group invitations others have sent you (if
any). The page also lists groups recently joined by your friends and
groups you've already joined that have updated information. To visit any
of the groups you see listed, simply click the group name to open its associated page.

FIGURE 10.2   The Groups application lists recently updated groups and
groups your friends have joined.

Browsing Groups

A great way to locate a group is to simply browse to see what's out there. Click the **Browse Groups** link at the top of the Groups page. This opens a page listing groups, as shown in Figure 10.3. Depending on what filters are turned on, the listings may show groups that are part of your network, locality network, or global network. You can scroll through to see the groups listed, or you can choose to view groups related to categories. The right side of the page features a category listing. Just click the one you like to view the associated groups.

FIGURE 10.3 You can browse groups based on category to see what sort of groups are out there.

To return to the main Groups page at any time, click the **Back to Groups** link at the top of the page.

Searching for a Group

You can use the search feature on the Groups page to look up a group. For example, if you want to find a group related to snow skiing in Colorado or a mom's group in your area, you can conduct a quick search and see what's available. There are groups centered around just about every subject you can think of, and many more you hadn't thought of at all.

To search for a particular group or topic, click in the **Search for Groups** field at the top of the Groups page. Type in the keyword or words you want to search for; then press **Enter** or **Return**.

Facebook displays any matches. The results page for groups lists the groups with a block of information detailing the group name, number of members, type of group, and new group activity. To view a group, click the group name to open its page. The group page tells you more about the group, and you can see what sort of activities they pursue.

To filter the display of results, click the **Show results from** drop-down arrow and choose a filter. You can also click the **Show More Filters** link to display a menu you can use to filter the list by categories.

The results page offers two tabs: All Results and Groups. By default, the **Groups** tab is active, listing results for groups and nothing else. To view all matches, including non-group matches such as profiles, fan pages, and so on, click the **All Results** tab. .

Joining a Group

You can join up to 300 groups on Facebook, so don't feel limited to just a few. After you find a group you like, join it and become a member. It's a good idea to check out the group page first just to see if it's something you really want to participate in, as shown in Figure 10.4. Group pages can include anything that regular profile pages can, including profile pictures, a Wall, posted links, photos and videos, and a listing of who manages the group. The group page also features a list of members of the group.

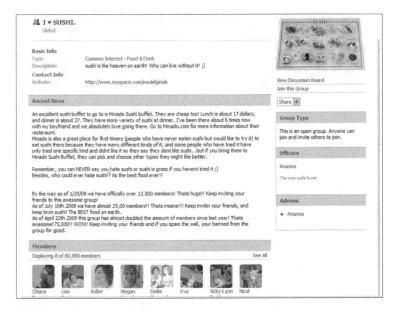

FIGURE 10.4 A typical group page.

Active groups have more Wall postings than less active groups, and really active groups have discussion boards going. Discussion boards are organized by topics, and users post comments, questions, and answers in an ongoing conversation. You can view the various postings to get an idea of how the group operates.

You should also check to see if the group has an active administrator. If there is no administrator, the group probably isn't thriving very much.

If you're ready to join, and it's an open group, look for the **Join this Group** link on the group's page. Click the link, and Facebook displays a prompt box, as shown in Figure 10.5. Click **Join** to immediately join and start participating in the group. If it's a closed group, you'll need to request membership from the administrator.

If the group is closed, you can join only if the administrator of the group allows you to; you'll have to request to join. Figure 10.6 shows an example of a closed group listing. You can click the **Request to Join** link to contact the administrator. Then you'll have to wait to hear back as to whether you're approved or not.

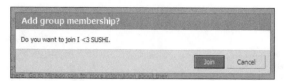

FIGURE 10.5   You must jump through one more box before actually joining a group.

FIGURE 10.6   You can tell closed groups by their "Request to Join" links.

Your friends will probably send you links from time to time to join their groups. Look for group requests among your Facebook requests. From the Home page, click the **See All** link in the Requests box in the upper-right corner to view all your Facebook requests. Scroll down the Requests page to view your group invitations. If you see something you want to join, click the **Confirm** button, as shown in Figure 10.7. Confirming a group works similarly to confirming a friend.

You can also view group invitations on the My Groups page. The next section shows you how to navigate to the page.

After you've joined a group, you can start participating. Communication in groups takes place mainly in two forms: the Wall or discussion boards. All group pages have a Wall, just like the Wall on your profile page, where members post comments. Look for the "Write Something" box to write on the group Wall.

Groups can also use *discussion boards*, which are topic-focused discussions. One person starts the discussion and others chime in. Discussion boards work similarly to Facebook's comments feature, but you're addressing the group when you type your reply, and it's posted on the board where others can add to it.

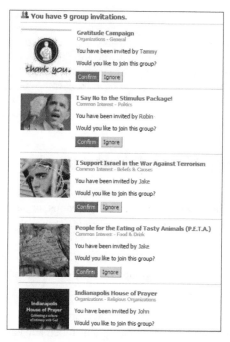

FIGURE 10.7   You can confirm or ignore group invitations from your friends.

When you do find a group you really like, and you think your Facebook friends might like it too, you can invite your friends to join the group. Look for the **Invite People to Join** link in the upper-right corner under the group profile picture on the group page.

Groups you join become stories on your profile page's mini-feed, and can also appear on the news feed on the Home page. You may also want to share news about the group at other times, and you can do so using the **Share** button on the group page. Click the **Share** button to open the Share dialog box, where you can share a posting about the group on your profile page or message a friend about the group. In either scenario, a link to the group appears, and others can click it to view the group.

> **Note**
> You can also find a list of groups you've joined on the Info tab of
> your profile page. Scroll down the Info tab page to view a Groups
> section among the various bits of information. Listed group names
> that appear also act as links you click to view the associated group
> page.

Viewing Your Groups

To view the groups you've joined, open the Groups application page
(click the **Applications** button; then click **Groups**, or just click the
Groups button found on the same Applications bar as the Applications
button). From there, you can click the **My Groups** link at the top to view
a page listing all your groups. Facebook displays the My Groups page.
The My Groups page shows groups you've joined, as well as groups to
which you've received invitations.

If you scroll to the very bottom of the My Groups page, as shown in
Figure 10.8, you'll find more group options for creating and searching for
groups. You can browse among the group categories and search for a particular group using the Search box. You can learn more about creating
new groups later in this lesson.

FIGURE 10.8   The bottom of the My Groups page has options for creating a
new group or browsing existing groups.

Here's what you can do on the My Groups page:

▶ You can scroll through your list of groups and click one to open its
  page.

▶ You can filter your groups based on recent updates, number of members, groups you're the administrator of, and groups you're invited to.

► You can also choose to leave a group at any time. Simply click
the **Leave Group** link on the My Groups page next to the group
name. You can also click this same link found on the group's
page.

► To decline an invitation to join a particular group, click the
Reject Invitation link.

► Scroll to the bottom of the page and click the **Create Group**
button to make your own group. Learn more about creating new
groups later in this lesson.

► To browse for a group based on a category, scroll to the bottom
and click a category link. This opens the Browse Groups page
you learned about earlier in this lesson.

► To search for a group, click in the **Search** box and type in a keyword or words; then press **Enter** or **Return**.

Starting Your Own Group

If you cannot find a group that suits your needs, you can create a new
group. You might also create a new group to serve a specific purpose,
such as a work group centered around a project, or a family group focused
just on your family members. Before you jump in and make a new group,
take a few minutes to figure out these details first:

► Decide what you want to name the group. You cannot change the
name after you've started the group, so make sure it has the
name you want, because you're stuck with it. Watch out for mis-
spellings and typos!

► Decide what photo you want to use as the group profile picture.
Try to choose an image that goes along with what the group is
about.

► Write out a brief description of the group, stating the group's
purpose, mission, or intent. This information is required in the
Create a Group form.

▶ Formulate an idea about what type of group you're creating, such as common interest, business related, or just for fun. A group type is required to categorize the group on Facebook. The form you use to create the group offers a drop-down list of choices, but it helps to have some idea up front to make the process easier.

▶ Decide on availability: open, closed, or secret. If the group is open, is it open to everyone (globally) or just those on your network?

▶ Decide what contact information you want to include, such as your email address, headquarters, or street address. Contact information is optional.

▶ Decide on what content you want to display on the page.

You'll save yourself some time and effort by organizing your group information before actually creating the group.

To start your own group, follow these steps:

1. Open the Groups application page (click the **Groups** button on the Applications bar or click the **Applications** button; then click **Groups**).

2. Click the **Create a New Group** button.

   The Create a Group page opens to the first step, shown in Figure 10.9—a form to fill out with details about your group.

3. Fill in the form details on the Step 1: Group Info page.

   You must fill in the required fields in order to proceed. All other fields are optional.

4. Click the **Create Group** button.

   The Step 2: Customize page appears, as shown in Figure 10.10, with options for uploading a group profile picture, associating a web page, deciding content display, and choosing group availability.

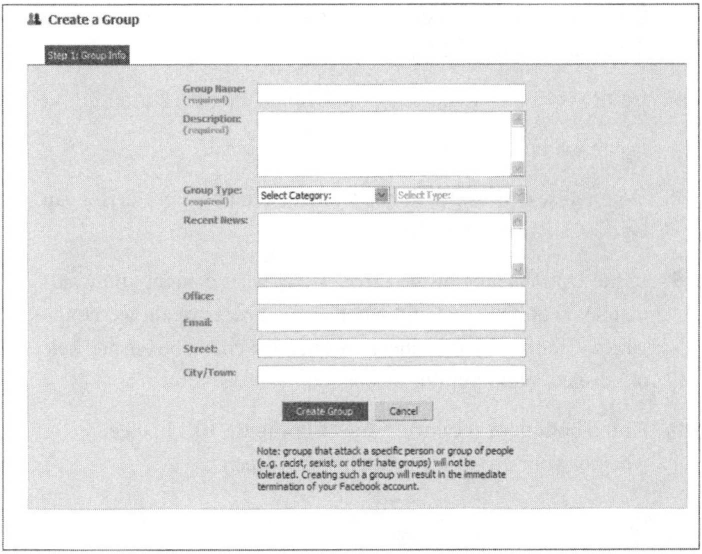

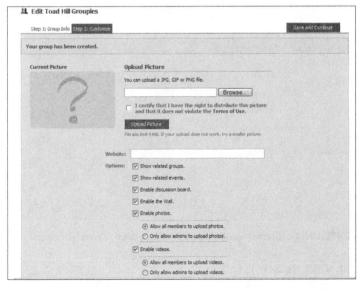

FIGURE 10.9 Fill out the form with a group name, description, and group type.

FIGURE 10.10 Use the Customize page to add a photo and customize the page content.

5. Click the **Browse** button to select and upload a photo to use as the group profile picture.

6. Certify the upload and click the **Upload Picture** button.

   Facebook uploads the image.

7. Optionally, if your group has an associated web page, you can type its URL in the Website box.

8. In the Options area of the form, select what content you want displayed on the page and whether members are allowed to post various items. You can check or uncheck check boxes and select or deselect radio buttons as needed.

9. At the bottom of the form, shown in Figure 10.11, specify whether your group is open, closed, or secret.

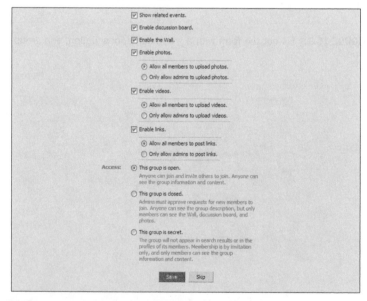

FIGURE 10.11   Choose an availability option: open, closed, or secret.

10. Click the **Save** button.

    Facebook asks you to publish the information as a story on your profile page and news feed.

11. Click **Publish** to publish the story, or **Skip** to skip the story for now.

Finally, the Invite Friends page appears, as shown in Figure 10.12. You can use this page to invite your friends to join the group.

FIGURE 10.12 The last part of creating a group is inviting friends.

12. Click the friends from your list who you want to invite, or type in the email addresses of friends outside of Facebook.

13. Optionally, add a personal message to the invitation.

14. Click the **Send Invitations** button at the bottom of the form.

Facebook displays a confirmation that the invites were sent. You can continue inviting more people, or exit and go view your new group page.

Managing Your Group

As the creator of a group, you're in charge of administrating the group. You're automatically given the title of administrator, also called admin for short on Facebook. You also have the default title of creator. It's your job to keep an eye out on the group and the content posted there by others, and keep the group alive and active. You can post news about the group, send out group messages to your members, and even assign officer positions. Basically, this is your club, and you're in charge of making everyone feel welcome and to encourage participation.

You can find links to tasks you can do to manage the group located directly below the group's profile picture, as shown in Figure 10.13. You can return to the form fields you originally filled out to create the group and make changes to the information.

FIGURE 10.13   Use the links on the group page to manage the group.

Here are a few management tasks you can do on your group's page:

▶ Click the **Edit Group** link underneath the group profile picture to open the same forms you used to create the group. You can edit the information within each tab, with the exception of changing the group name. For example, you can use the Recent News field (Group Info tab) to create a News box on the group page and list the latest news about the group. Don't forget to click the **Save Changes** button to save any changes.

▶ To add more administrators to the group, click the **Edit Members** link. This opens the Edit Members page, where you can use the **Make Admin** button to assign administrator duties to any member.

▶ To add officer positions, click the **Edit Group** link; then click the **Officers** tab and assign honorary titles or officer positions to select members.

▶ To add a discussion group topic, click the **Start New Topic** link under the discussion board heading; then type in a topic and post a comment. Click the **Post new topic** button to add the discussion topic to the board. If it's the first topic to be added to the discussion, the link is labeled **Start the first topic**.

▶ To send a group email message, click the **Message All Members** link and type up your group email message.

▶ For a fee, you can advertise your group on Facebook. Click the **Promote Group with an Ad** link to learn more.

▶ To invite more people to your group, click the **Invite People to Join** link.

▶ You can also create events for your group. See Lesson 11, "Tracking Events," to learn more about this Facebook feature.

Note

When you create a group-related event, it shows up on the group's page and all the group members are invited to attend.

Along with the management activities described previously, you can also administer the postings on the Wall and among the topics on the discussion board:

▶ To remove a post from the Wall, click the **Delete** link located directly below the posting, then click the **Delete** button to confirm the deletion.

- ▶ To remove a post from a discussion topic, open the topic and then click the **Delete Post** link.

- ▶ To remove a topic entirely, click the **Delete Topic** link.

Finally, you may run into a problem with an unruly member in your group. You can certainly address that member privately in an email, and you can also remove him or her from your group entirely. To do so, click the **Edit Members** link; then click the **X** button next to the group member's name.

Tip

To delete your group from Facebook, first remove all the members and then click the **Leave Group** link. If you prefer to exit the group yourself but leave it active and give it to someone else to manage, you can click the **Leave Group** link, and Facebook offers the position to any of the remaining members.

Summary

In this lesson, you learned how to utilize groups on Facebook. You learned how to look for groups to join, how to manage the groups you do join, and how to create brand-new groups and act as administrator. In the next lesson, you learn how to use Facebook events.

LESSON 11

Tracking Events

In this lesson, you learn how to find and create Facebook events. You learn how to search for events in your area and handle event invitations. You also learn how to create your own events and manage their pages.

Events Overview

Events are another amazing social aspect of using Facebook. You can quickly get the word out among your friends and interested others about upcoming events, whether it's a party, a concert, a trip, or any other kind of social gathering. For example, if you're organizing a rally of some sort, you can turn it into a Facebook event to let everyone know about it and invite people to attend and spread the word, thus increasing your chances of a good crowd. In another example, a friend of a friend might be having a backyard barbecue, and you don't know whether you want to go or not. You can check the attendees list to see if anyone else you know is going. Facebook events are perfect for sending out informal invitations and planning out your social itinerary.

You can use Facebook's Events application to advertise an event, track attendees, view birthdays, and find other events. The application is one of several default applications already loaded into your Facebook account. You can use the application to search for events in your area, or create new events yourself. The Events application acts as your personal secretary when it comes to your social calendar.

You can use the Events application to create all kinds of events, including numerous types of parties, fundraisers, meetings, educational classes or study groups, exhibits, recitals, sporting events and tournaments, trips, and festivals. Events you create using the Events application have their own

pages on Facebook. The person who creates the event page in Facebook is
the page's administrator and controls the content and management of the
event page. An event page, shown in Figure 11.1, looks like a group page
and features information about the event itself. It has an area listing
details and a description, an event "profile" picture area, a Wall for posting comments, and features for tracking who's attending and how to
RSVP.

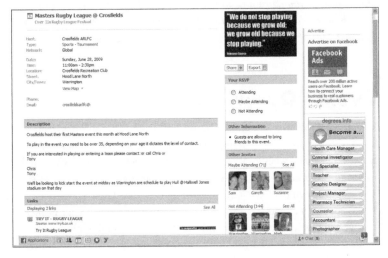

FIGURE 11.1   An example of a typical event page on Facebook.

Facebook events come in three different types, as follows:

Open Events   Anyone can read about an open event and accept an
invitation to attend it. Open events are perfect for festivals, gallery
showings, concerts, and other large public gatherings.

Closed Events   Only the people you invite can choose to attend a
closed event. Others can read about the event, but you cannot attend
without an invitation.

Secret Events   This event is completely secret except to the people you invite.

Whether you can attend an event or not depends on how it is listed. Look in the Event Type area of the page to see what type of event it is.

There are also a few things to keep in mind when attending Facebook events in person. Meeting people online and meeting them face-to-face are both situations in which you should always use common sense coupled with caution. Just because someone appears to be one way online doesn't mean he or she will be the same in person. Online dangers can often be avoided by following secure habits (antivirus software, privacy settings, passwords, and so on); however, when you meet people in real life, criminal behaviors can take physical shape. Just be careful!

Finding Events

Ready to find something fun to do? Or how about seeing what your friends are attending? There are several ways to find out about an event. One way is to check the news feed on the Home page to see what events your friends are attending. You can also browse listed events in your area. Finally, you can search for specific events.

You can use the Events application to look up events to attend. To access the app, just click the **Applications** button and click **Events**, as shown in Figure 11.2, or click the **Events** button on the same Application bar.

Facebook opens the Events page (see Figure 11.2), listing tabs of event activities you can view, as follows:

> **Upcoming Events**   Lists all the events you've been invited to or have agreed to attend.
>
> **Friends' Events**   Lists all the events your friends are planning to attend.
>
> **Past Events**   Displays an archive of previous events.
>
> **Birthdays**   Displays all your Facebook friends with upcoming birthdays.

You can click a tab name to view the listings.

FIGURE 11.2   Use the Events application to view events.

At the top of the Events page are links for browsing events and for exporting your events to another scheduling program, such as Microsoft Outlook or Google Calendar. Also at the top of the page is a Search box for looking for an event and a **Create an Event** button for making your own event listings.

Browsing Events

You can use the **Browse Events** linkon the Events page to see what sort of activities are out there on your network. Click the **Browse Events** link to open the Browse Events page, similar to Figure 11.3. This page lists any upcoming events. Depending on your network, the search results may list many pages or just a few. You can use the **Filters** on the right side of the page to filter how the events appear. For example, you can filter the list to show only tomorrow's events, or only sports events. Simply click a drop-down list and choose a filter. You can filter the results by network, date, or type.

When you find an event you want to learn more about, click the event name to open the event page, as shown in Figure 11.4. Here you can read more about the event, who is hosting the event, and details about the time and place. In the case of open events, you can also RSVP.

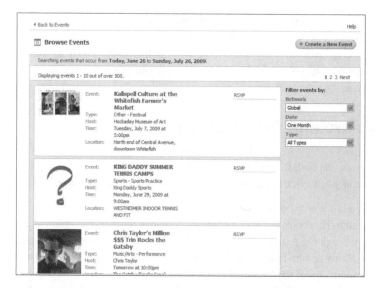

FIGURE 11.3 You can browse events and find out what's available in your area.

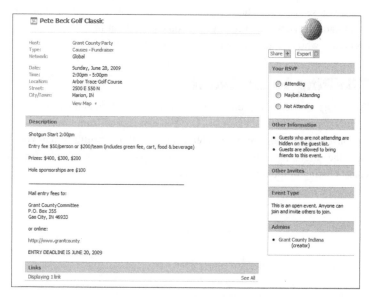

FIGURE 11.4 If you find an event you want to attend, select an RSVP option.

Be sure to read the page carefully regarding whether extra guests are allowed. You can also share this event with others by clicking the **Share** button to open the Share dialog box. You can then post the link to the event on your profile page and news feed, or you can message someone a link to the event.

Searching for an Event

If you know the event you're looking for, either by name or subject, you can use the built-in search tool to look it up. To conduct a search from the Events page, click in the **Search for Events** box at the top of the page.

Type in the word or words you want to search for and press **Enter** or **Return**. Facebook displays a page with any matching results. You can filter through the results page using the filters at the top. For example, click the **Show results from** drop-down menu and choose a network. You can also further sort the list based on the date or event type using the **Show More Filters** link. When you click this link, Facebook displays more filters to choose from for sorting the list.

When you see an event that matches what you want, you can click on the event name to view the event's page. You can find out more about the event, see who is attending, and locate a link to RSVP yourself.

RSVPing to an Event

To sign up to attend an event, you can click an RSVP option on the event's page, as shown in Figure 11.5. You can choose from three responses: **Attending**, **Maybe Attending**, or **Not Attending**. When you click the Attending response, Facebook adds you to the event's Confirmed Guests listing in the middle of the page.

FIGURE 11.5   Select an RSVP option to let the administrator know if you're attending.

You might also receive a personal invitation to attend an event. Invites appears as requests among your Facebook requests. To view your event requests, you can display the Requests page. From the Home page, click the invitations link in the upper-right corner in the Requests area, as shown in Figure 11.6. Facebook opens your Requests page. You can also click the **See All** link and then scroll down the page to the Event Requests area and see what you need to respond to.

FIGURE 11.6 One way to find out about your event invitations is through the Requests area on your Home page.

Click an event name to learn more about the event, or you can respond directly by clicking the **Yes** button, the **Maybe** button, or the **No** button, as shown in Figure 11.7. You can use the **RSVP** box to send back a message along with your attendance selection. To remove the event entirely from your listings, click the **Remove from My Events** link.

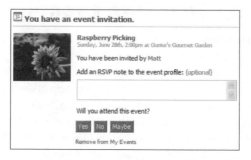

FIGURE 11.7 You can RSVP from the Requests page.

Events you are invited to also show up on your Events page on the **Upcoming Events** tab.

You can RSVP to the event by clicking the **RSVP** link. This opens a box, shown in Figure 11.8, which you can use to send back a reply. Choose

from **Attending**, **Maybe Attending**, or **Not Attending** and click the
RSVP button.

FIGURE 11.8   The RSVP box.

You can also change an RSVP response from the Events page. For example, if it turns out that you cannot attend the event, just click the **Edit** link
to open the same RSVP box and change your selection.

Depending on how the event's administrator has the page set up, you may
be able to view all the people who have accepted an invitation to the
event, as well as those who are thinking about attending. If you've agreed
to attend the event, your name and picture also appear in the listing.

Creating Your Own Events

You can create your own events and invite others to join you. Events run
the full gamut from public gatherings to intimate parties. For example, if
you're part of a group organizing a fun run race or other fundraising
event, you can create a Facebook event for your network or area and
invite people to attend. After people start RSVPing, their friends see the
event, and they think about attending, too. It's great word of mouth about
your group and your cause. Facebook events are perfect for advertising
festivals, flea markets, gallery openings, holiday parties, business meetings, conventions, piano recitals, tournaments, workshops, and so on.

Events are also categorized for easy sorting. When someone creates an
event, they must assign a category type, as follows:

▶ Party

▶ Causes

- ▶ Education
- ▶ Meetings
- ▶ Music/Arts
- ▶ Sports
- ▶ Trips
- ▶ Other

Each category has a subcategory to further define the event. For example, if you create a party event, you can then pinpoint what type of party it is, such as birthday, cocktail, or goodbye party.

Before you begin creating a new event, take a moment and figure out the details you'll need for posting the event. Required data includes a name for the event, a type and subcategory for the event, the host's name, and a location. You cannot create an event without this information. You'll also need some basic information, such as time and date. Although it's not a requirement, it's a good idea to have a picture handy to go along with your event page—something that illustrates what the event is about or the organization hosting the event.

When you're ready to create an event, follow these steps:

1. Open the Events application (click the **Events** button on the Applications bar or click the **Applications** button; then click **Events**).

2. Click the **Create an Event** button.

   Facebook displays step 1 of the process, which is a form page you can fill out with details about the event, as shown in Figure 11.9.

3. Fill out the form's details, as needed. Required fields are marked as such on the form.

4. Click the **Create Event** button at the bottom of the form.

   Facebook displays step 2 of the process, shown in Figure 11.10—another form page for adding a picture and setting options for page content and whether the page is open, closed, or secret.

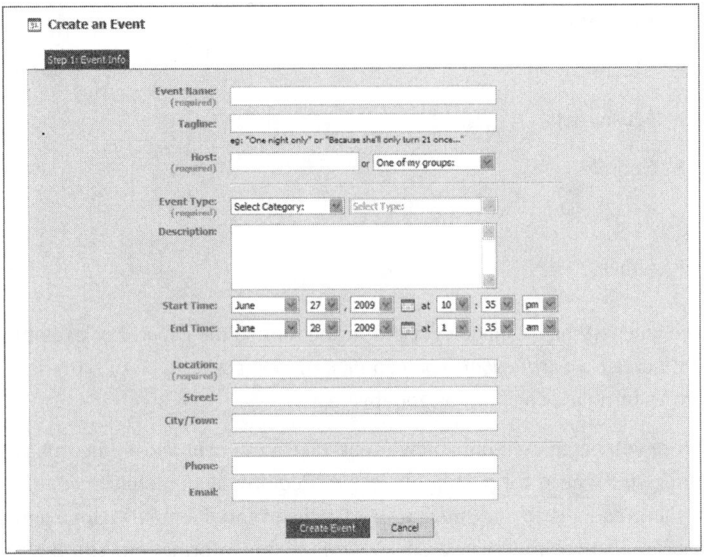

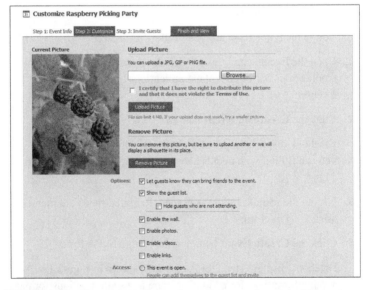

FIGURE 11.9   The first phase of creating a new event is filling out this form page.

FIGURE 11.10   The second phase of creating a new event is filling out a second form page.

5. Fill out the second form's details, as needed.

To add a picture, click the **Browse** button, locate and double-click the picture you want to use, authorize the distribution using the **I certify that I have the right to distribute this picture** check box, and then click the **Upload** button.

To add or hide page content, check or uncheck the boxes for displaying guests, the Wall, links, photos, or videos.

Select an access setting: **Open**, **Closed**, or **Secret**.

Optionally, if you want the event publicized in the search results, click the **Show this event in search results** check box.

6. Click the **Save** button to continue.

7. Facebook asks to publish the event on your profile page and news feed. Click **Publish** to agree, or click **Skip** to forgo the posting.

Facebook displays step 3 of the process, shown in Figure 11.11—a final form for selecting people to invite.

FIGURE 11.11 The final phase of creating a new event is inviting friends.

8. Fill out the final form as needed.

Select the guests from your friends list who you want to invite.

You can click the **Filter Friends** menu to filter the list by network or Friend List.

You can also invite people not on Facebook by typing in their email addresses.

To include a personal invitation, you can type something in the **Personal Message** box.

9. Click **Send Invitations**.

Facebook sends out notifications regarding the event, and lets you know at the top of the page. The event now also appears on your My Events page.

You can continue inviting more people or click the event's link in the upper-right corner, **Back to ... name of event**, to view the event's page.

Managing Your Events

After you've created an event, you're automatically the administrator of the event page. This means you can edit the page's info, make changes to the guest list, and send out more invitations as needed.

To view the page at any time, open the Events page (click the **Events** button or click the **Applications** button and then click **Events**). The event appears listed in your **Upcoming Events** tab (see Figure 11.12). The listing also includes some extra links for you as the administrator.

Here's what you can do with the extra admins links:

▶ To edit the page, simply click the **Edit Event** link, as shown in Figure 11.12. This opens the same form, with tabs, you used to create the event, and you can make changes to the information. One thing you cannot change is the event name.

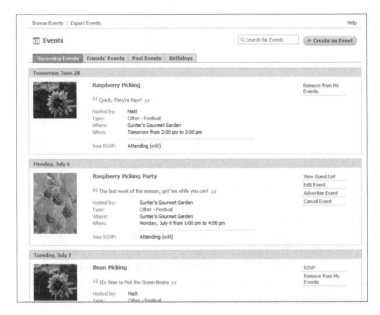

FIGURE 11.12   You can use the My Events page to view your events.

▶ To view the guests who have responded to your event invitation, click the **View Guest List** link.

▶ To advertise your event on Facebook for a fee, click the **Advertise Event** link and follow the instructions.

▶ To cancel the event, click the **Cancel Event** link to open the form shown in Figure 11.13. You can fill out a message about why you're cancelling, and Facebook sends a message to everyone on your guest list. Cancelling is a one-time deal—you cannot undo it and un-cancel the event again.

TIP

If your event is related to your group page, you can connect the two so the event shows up on the group page. To do so, open the group page and click the **Create Related Event** link.

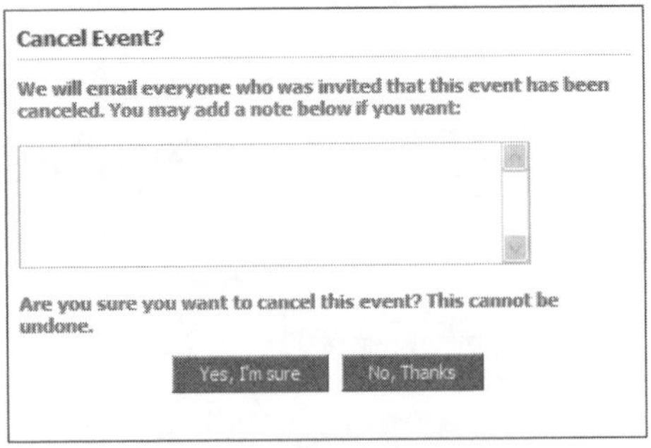

FIGURE 11.13   Cancelling an event is permanent.

You can continue monitoring your event page leading up to the event, checking to see who is attending, not attending, or thinking about attending, and viewing any page content left by the invitees. You can send out messages to the attendees. You can also update the page with the latest news about the event as it draws near. .

Summary

In this lesson, you learned how to find and create events on Facebook. You learned how to look for events to attend, and how to create a new event and invite your friends. You also learned how to respond to RSVPs and administer an event page. In the next lesson, you'll learn how to use Facebook applications.

LESSON 12

Adding Applications

In this lesson, you learn how to use applications to enhance your Facebook experience. You'll learn how to search for applications and add interesting ones to your collection. You'll also learn how to manage your applications, edit their settings, and remove apps you no longer want.

Applications Overview

Applications are tiny programs that run within the Facebook environment—also called *apps* for short. Applications are rather like plug-ins you use to enhance your web browser, but in the case of Facebook, they enhance your social networking experiences. You've already been using applications on Facebook, perhaps without even knowing it, and we've covered quite a few so far in this book. This section will go into them with a bit more detail.

As you know, Facebook has several default applications going as soon as you create your account. If you've used Facebook to post your status, upload a photo or video, create a group or event, post a note, or chat, you've used a Facebook application. Apps work seamlessly within the Facebook interface.

Facebook's designers have included many useful built-in apps, but there are literally hundreds of applications you can add to your Facebook experience. Some are quite useful, and some are just for fun. Some you can add to your profile page, as shown in Figure 12.1, whereas others work on their own pages. These additional applications are created by third-party developers. Facebook has allowed third-party developers free access to the Facebook platform for several years now, so anyone who has some programming experience or wherewithal can write an application for the site.

Because of this freedom, Facebook is literally swarming with apps, and many of them are quite clever and creative. You can use as many as you like, and discard those you do not care for after giving them a whirl. All the extra apps you add, however, require your authorization to access your Facebook profile data. In many respects, adding an application is like adding a friend to your friends list. Apps are part of your Facebook account until you discard them. In many cases, apps like to publish your application activities on your profile page and news feed. This lets your friends know what applications you use and might inspire them to use them, too—all part of the viral spread of apps on Facebook.

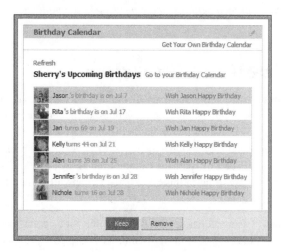

FIGURE 12.1   Here's an example of the Birthday Calendar app I added to my profile page.

When you add apps to your Facebook account, you can add them as separate tabs on your profile page (depending on the app). For example, you can add a tab for the Photos app which you learned about back in Lesson 8, or a tab for the SuperPoke aoo. This is handy if you use the application frequently and want easy access to it. Some apps can also appear in their own boxed area on your profile page, such as the Birthday Calendar app shown in Figure 12.1

> **CAUTION**
> When you allow an application access to your profile, it accesses all your information and that of your friends, too. If you're worried about privacy, applications may not be your cup of tea. For this very reason, you may not want to include too much personal information on your Facebook pages. (To learn more about privacy settings, see Lesson 5, "Guarding Your Privacy.") You can, however, control some of the invasiveness of apps through the application's settings. Learn more about editing apps later in this lesson.

Kinds of Apps

At this point, you may be wondering what kinds of things apps offer. There are a wide variety of applications, ranging from business and education to fun and games. For example, culture-sharing apps let you share information about things you like with your friends and they with you, such as musical tastes, books you just read, or movie reviews. Friendship apps include applications designed to organize and interact with friends. Self-expression apps let you express your personality on your profile page, such as adding pieces of flair (see Figure 12.2) or graffiti, whereas game apps let you play interactive or single-player games.

One of the more popular apps is We're Related, brought to you by FamilyLink, an application to help you locate and connect with relatives around the globe. Another popular application just for fun is Wordscraper, an inventive word game you can play. Some apps create digital worlds where you can interact with others, such as YoVille (see Figure 12.3) or Mafia Wars (both created by Zynga games), whereas others enhance a popular Facebook activity, such as Birthday Calendar (tracking birthdays), Extended Info (adding more information to your profile page), or NetworkedBlogs (blogging).

FIGURE 12.2 Express yourself with Flair buttons on a digital corkboard that you can add to your profile page.

FIGURE 12.3 In YoVille, you can wander around a digital world collecting coins and shopping for stuff for your digital dwelling, as well as interacting with your Facebook friends who also exist in YoVille.

Using the Applications Bar

You can use the Applications bar at the bottom of the browser window to create bookmarks, or *shortcuts*, to your favorite apps. The bar already includes icons for accessing Photos, Video, Groups, Events, Notes, and Links,. You can add more application icons as desired. The Applications menu, shown in Figure 12.4, also lists your applications. You can click the button to display the menu and then click the application you want to use. The top of the menu lists apps you've recently used, and the rest of the menu lists your application bookmarks.

FIGURE 12.4   Use Facebook's Applications bar to access application shortcuts or display a menu of your apps.

Now that you know a little about what apps can do, it's time to start finding some you can use.

Finding Apps

You can encounter applications in several ways on Facebook. A friend may send you an app request, such as a game application in which they invite you to play or interact with them or a "gift" you must then use the application to view. Application requests typically occur when a friend adds a new application to their repertoire, and it asks to add you as well, because you're on their friends list. Application requests show up in the Requests area of your Home page (top-right corner).

You can also encounter apps on other people's profile pages and news feeds and choose to add the application to your profile, too. If you see something you think you'd like, you can click the application name in the story posting to learn more about the application.

Finally, you can use Facebook's Application Directory to browse for apps or look for specific ones to learn more about them. The Application Directory, itself an application, lets you browse for apps based on category or by name.

Deciding which apps are right for you is really a personal preference. Many of the Facebook apps are viral, quickly spreading in popularity as they're shared among friends—your friend adds the application, it looks interesting, so you add it, too. If you see an app you think you'd like to try, you can check out its page first to learn more about it and find out which of your friends is using the app.

> TIP
> When determining whether an app is trustworthy or not, look for the Facebook Verified App badge and check mark that appears on the apps page. This check mark means the application has passed Facebook's review process for complying with Facebook's terms of service and standards, and are believed to be trustworthy for keeping your information safe.

Responding to an App Request

Basically, an application request is when an app invites you to participate in whatever it's about, or when your friend who uses the app wants to invite you to use it, too. When you receive an application request, it appears in the upper-right corner of your Home page. You can click the request, or you can click the **See All** link and view the entire Requests page, as shown in Figure 12.5. Scroll down the Requests page to view your application requests.

FIGURE 12.5   You can respond to application requests on the Requests page.

The request presents several options for responding. The first option, though it may have different names, is essentially a button you can click to join, accept, or participate. When clicked, additional pages may open where you can allow the application to access your data. The second option is to ignore the request. When you click the **Ignore** button, the request is removed from the Requests page.

If you prefer to learn more about the application before choosing a response, you can visit the apps info or "profile" page and learn more about it. Similar to a profile page, an application's page has a Wall for comments and tabs for info, reviews, and discussion boards, and even a "profile picture." Click the application name in the request title area to display the information page.

As you can see in Figure 12.5, there are also several links below the request information to block the application from inviting you again, or block all application requests from the friend who sent it to you. You might find these handy if your friend persistently sends you unwelcomed invites to apps you'll never use. If you click the **Ignore All Invites From This Friend** link, the friend never finds out about your decision, and you can end the parade of requests. If you click the **Block This Application** link, you can prevent the application from contacting you again, ever. Unless you reactivate the application again at a later time.

Browsing Apps with the Application Directory

With literally hundreds of apps to choose from, finding apps is easy. To see what kind of apps are available on Facebook, you can open the Application Directory and browse to your hearts content. To display the directory, click the **Applications** button on the Applications bar at the bottom of the browser window; this opens the menu. The menu lists your currently loaded applications. Click **Browse More Applications**.

Facebook opens the Application Directory, as shown in Figure 12.6. Click the **All Applications** category if it's not already selected by default. The Directory page lists categories of applications on the left, and suggestions for applications on the right, including featured apps. The **Recent Activity From Friends** section lists recent apps your friends have loaded. To peruse a category, select a category name on the left, such as **Business** or **Lifestyle**. Facebook then lists associated apps based on popularity.

FIGURE 12.6   The Application Directory page.

The Application Directory lists apps by category. The categories are pretty self-explanatory, as follows:

- ► Business
- ► Education
- ► Entertainment
- ► Friends & Family
- ► Games
- ► Just for Fun
- ► Lifestyle
- ► Sports
- ► Utilities

To view a category, simply click its name. The categories list on the left side of the page also has options for viewing other application types, as follows:

All Applications   Lists all the applications Facebook thinks you might like by clicking this option.

External Websites   View apps based on other sites.

Desktop   View apps geared toward desktop usage, such as apps for Twitter or Google.

Mobile   View apps available for Facebook's mobile features.

On Facebook   Lists featured apps, apps Facebook thinks you might like, and recent apps your friends are using.

When you choose a category to view, the applications listing includes a brief description of the apps and user review rankings measured by a star point system. The more stars an application receives indicates the more people like the application. The bottom of the description also lets you know how many monthly active users access the application and how many friends you have already using it. To learn more about a particular application, click its name. Facebook opens its associated profile page, as shown in Figure 12.7.

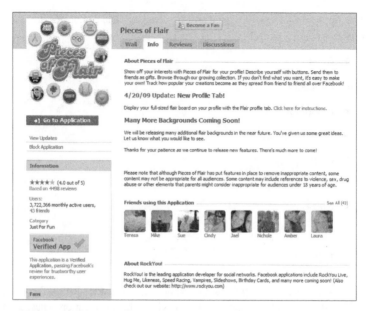

FIGURE 12.7   Each application has a page describing the app and a link for adding it to your Facebook account.

You can read more about the application, who designed it, reviews of the app, and even which of your friends are using it. Depending on the application, the page may display tabs for viewing additional information, a discussion board, and a Wall for posting comments. To add the app to your repertoire, click the **Go To Application** button. Depending on the app, the Allow Access page may appear, similar to Figure 12.8. Click the **Allow** button to continue and add the app. Click the **Cancel** link to forgo the procedure.

FIGURE 12.8   Before adding an application, you must first officially approve its access to your information.

Searching for Apps

You can also conduct a keyword search to look for a specific application. On the Application Directory page, click inside the **Search Apps** box. Type in the keyword or words you want to search for and press **Enter** or **Return**. Facebook conducts a search and displays any resulting matches.

The Search Results page include a brief description of the app, a review rating, the number of active monthly users, and the number of friends who use the app. From the list of matches, you can click an application name to view its associated page of information and add the application to your Facebook account.

TIP

If you'd like to learn how to create your own apps for Facebook, you can check out the Developers page for more information, tips, and help. Click the **Developers** link at the bottom of any Facebook page to open the page.

Managing Applications

After you've added an application, you can use it as much or as little as you like. Depending on the app, you can change how it's accessed or where it appears on your Facebook profile page. Not all apps are profile-based, but you can always access them through the Applications menu. The application's name is automatically added to the **Applications** menu (click the **Applications** button in the lower-left corner of the browser window to see a list of your applications) by default. Some apps even let you put a bookmark icon on the Applications bar itself for quicker access.

Changing Application Settings

You can edit your applications through the Application Settings page, shown in Figure 12.9. To navigate to the page, click the **Applications** button and then click **Edit Applications**. You can also find your way to the page by moving the mouse pointer over the **Settings** link in the navigation bar and then clicking **Application Settings**.

The Application Settings page lists each of the applications you are using. You can use the **Show** drop-down list to filter the apps display. You can show recently used apps, bookmarked apps, apps that are added to your profile page, authorized apps, allowed to post apps, and granted additional permissions apps.

Application Settings - Recently Used

Displaying 15 applications you have used in the past month.   Show: Recently Used

Addicted to Firefly	Edit Settings	Profile	X
Birthday Calendar	Edit Settings	Profile	X
Events	Edit Settings	Profile	X
Gifts	Edit Settings	Profile	X
Groups	Edit Settings	Profile	X
How Well Do You Know Me?	Edit Settings	Profile	X
Marketplace	Edit Settings	Profile	X
Notes	Edit Settings	Profile	X
Photos	Edit Settings	Profile	X
Links	Edit Settings	Profile	X
Slide FunSpace	Edit Settings	Profile	X
SuperPoke!	Edit Settings	Profile	X
Video	Edit Settings	Profile	X
What color are you?	Edit Settings	Profile	X
YoVille	Edit Settings	Profile	X

FIGURE 12.9   The Application Settings page.

To edit an application, click the **Edit Settings** link. This opens a Settings dialog box similar to Figure 12.10, with tabs for changing the application's settings. Depending on the application, you can use the tabs to change privacy settings, add a bookmark, or control how related stories are generated when using the application. For example, if the application offers a **Profile** tab, you can click the **Privacy** drop-down list and choose who can view your activities with the application. If the application offers an **Additional Permissions** tab, you can control the display of related stories on the news feed and on your profile page's mini-feed. Click **Okay** to save any changes you make to the settings.

To view more information about the application, click the **Profile** link.
This takes you to the app's profile page where you can view its description and rating, see which friends are using it, post comments on the Wall,
and more.

FIGURE 12.10   You can edit individual settings for your apps to change
how they work.

Removing Apps

You can remove an application you no longer want or are no longer using.
You might also remove applications to clean up your list just as a mainte-
nance task. To delete an app, first open the Application Settings page as
described in the previous section. Next, click the Delete link (the X button
to the right of the application name). A prompt box appears. Click the
Remove button to delete the application. Optionally, and depending on
the application, you can rate the application or state a reason as to why
you're removing it.

One more prompt box appears to let you know the application is gone.
Click **Okay** to finish the process.

Displaying Apps

Some apps let you display a tab for them on your profile page for easy
access. To add a tab, open your profile page and click the **Add a New
Tab** tab—the one that looks like a plus sign (see Figure 12.11). Next,
click the name of the application you want to add. Facebook immediately
adds it to the list of tabs on the page. To remove it again, you can open

the apps Edit Settings dialog box; click the **Profile** tab and click the
Remove link next to the **Tab** option. For quicker removal, you can also
click the app's tab and a pencil icon appears next to the tab name. Click
the icon, then click **Delete Tab**.

FIGURE 12.11   You can add a tab for the application on your profile page.

Other apps let you add a box for them on the profile page on the Wall tab,
thus creating their own little space on the page, or on the Boxes tab. You
can open the application's Edit Settings dialog box to look for such an
option. Look in the **Profile** tab for a link next to the **Box** option; click **Add**.

Some apps let you place a bookmark for the app on the Applications bar.
Again, you can check the app's Edit Settings dialog box for such an
option.

> **TIP**
>
> You can rearrange applications shown on the Applications menu by
> dragging them to a new location on the menu list. Click the
> **Applications** button; then click and drag the app name to move it.

Summary

In this lesson, you learned how to use applications on Facebook. You
learned how to find applications, search for applications, and add applications to your Facebook account. You also learned how to manage your
apps. In the next lesson, you'll learn how to create Facebook pages.

LESSON 13

The Professional Side of Facebook: Pages

In this lesson, you learn how to promote a business, brand, or public figure using Facebook Pages. You'll learn the differences between regular profile pages, groups, and specialty Pages. You'll also learn how to subscribe to Pages, create your own Page, and manage it as its administrator.

Understanding Facebook Pages

If you represent a company, organization, or professional group of some kind, you can create a presence on Facebook. Unlike individual profile pages, however, you need to create a special page—one that starts with a capital P. Facebook *Pages* are designed specifically for professional use and are completely separate from profile pages. A Page is a great way for fans to find you or your brand and spread the word about upcoming events, news, and information. Pages are a tool for connecting directly with customers or an audience, and even attracting future fans or buyers. Facebook members can choose to be fans or supporters of Pages.

Pages are an ideal public relations/marketing tool for the following:

▶ Public figures, such as politicians and government officials

▶ Celebrities

▶ Bands and musicians

▶ Artists

▶ Non-profit organizations and charities

- ▶ Government agencies

- ▶ Large and small businesses

- ▶ Entertainment industries, such as television and radio

- ▶ Educational entities, such as schools, colleges, and universities

- ▶ Brand names and products, and the companies behind them

By using Pages, businesses, artists, and brands can interact with fans directly, going beyond one-directional conversation to dynamic communication. The content you post on a Page shows up in the news feeds of any fans or supporters, which in turn can be viewed by their friends, potentially driving up traffic to your Page and more customers to your door. As a marketing tool, Facebook Pages can help you increase product or brand awareness and interest, plus allow you more ways to communicate your message and receive feedback.

Pages, Profiles, or Groups?

Facebook users are often confused about the difference between profiles, groups, and Pages. There are certainly a lot of similarities between the three; for example, Facebook features, such as the Wall, are readily available in each. Take a look at this Page for beverage giant, Dr. Pepper, shown in Figure 13.1.

At first glance, the Page looks like a regular profile page. It has a Wall for posting comments, a profile picture, and tabs with other Facebook features. Although it looks like a profile page, it's actually much more. To help you distinguish between Pages, profiles, and groups, however, take a look at some of the differences:

- ▶ Any individual can create a profile page, but only an authorized representative can create a professional Page. If you're not an authorized representative, you can create a group for the person or entity instead and invite other fans to participate. See Lesson 10, "Joining Groups," to learn more.

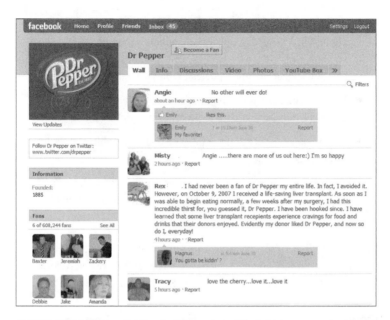

FIGURE 13.1   A Page for the Dr. Pepper brand soft drink.

▶ Pages are also different in that you don't see who is actually administering the content. No one's name, other than the company or public figure, appears on the Pages.

▶ With a Page, you don't have to okay friend requests on a Page. Anyone who wants to be a fan is automatically approved. This saves an administrator valuable time.

▶ Pages cannot invite people to be friends, rather, you can become a fan of a Page.

▶ Pages can integrate applications, contrasting with groups, which cannot add apps. With Pages, you can add apps such as Flash Player for uploading Flash files, YouTube Box to import your YouTube videos, or Simply RSS to import feeds.

▶ Unlike a regular profile page, a Page offers special administrator tools for collecting traffic and demographic information.

▶ A Page administrator can send out updates to every fan or supporter, but a group administrator can only send out messages to a
maximum of 5,000 members at most. Updates are like messages,
but they appear in your Updates tab in your Inbox.

▶ If you become a fan or supporter of a Page, the Page's administrator does not have access to your profile information.

▶ When you create a Page, it's indexed and searchable both inside
and outside of Facebook.

▶ Tools for creating profiles and groups are readily available; however, tools for creating professional Pages are more difficult to
locate on the site.

Basically, a Page is for promoting an entity or public figure, whereas a
profile is just for individuals. Groups are informal fan-created pages,
whereas Pages are authorized by the artist or company.

Strategies for Marketing with Pages

From a marketing standpoint, creating a Facebook Page for a business or
public figure can really generate ongoing buzz about a product or promo-
tion. One of the unique things about Pages is that you, as the administrator, can determine what tab on the Page users land on when they display
your Page. You can use this strategy to direct a user to a specific ad cam-
paign or action found on a custom tab on your Page. Take a look at Figure
13.2 for an example. It's a Page for world-famous Pizza Hut restaurants
with a custom tab touting their latest special.

Like the custom tab shown here, you can integrate all kinds of applications to engage the people who visit your Page. There are hundreds of
business-related apps you can use to help you create all kinds of interesting and interactive content. For example, you can create quizzes, surveys,
and games that keep users coming back for more. You can hold drawings
and contests to bring back people frequently to the Page. Be sure to keep
your Page content up-to-date and relevant. Utilize Facebook events to
reach out to your fan base and let them know about upcoming calendar
dates, engagements, concerts, rallies, or appearances.

FIGURE 13.2 A Page for Pizza Hut with a customized content tab displayed.

As far as communication goes, it's also a good strategy to respond promptly to fans who write on the Wall. Respond in kind by writing on their Wall. If someone comments on a photo or video, keep the dialogue going. Fans and supporters want to hear back from you, and this medium is designed just for this type of activity. A discussion board is also an excellent way to communicate with fans and create more interest. Start new threads regularly and encourage participation. Failing to engage your fans and supporters results in lost opportunities to generate revenue and interest. Remember, Facebook is a social network first and foremost, designed to foster human interaction. Your marketing strategy should focus on this, too, to help extend your brand or message.

NOTE

You can find numerous resources on the Internet to help you tap into the marketing and programming sides of Facebook, creating specialized apps and integrating others to suit your marketing needs. Sites like All Facebook (www.allfacebook.com) and Mashable (http://mashable.com) can offer some insights to get you started. Also be sure to check out Facebook's Developers page, too, by clicking the Developers link at the bottom of any Facebook page.

Finding and Following Pages

From a fan or supporter standpoint, you can subscribe to a Page and get regular updates whenever new information is published. News appears as a story on the news feed on your Home page. Actually finding Pages to become a fan of takes a little effort on your part. One way to find a Page you like is to stumble across a story about one on your friends' mini-feeds on their profile pages. Check their profile pages and see what Pages they're subscribing to or what public figures they're supporting. Simply click the link in the story to view the Page yourself.

You can also conduct a search for a particular name or product and see what's available on Facebook. Click in the **Search** box at the top of any Facebook page in the navigation bar and type in the keyword or words you're searching for, such as a company or product name. Press **Enter** or **Return**, and Facebook displays any matches on a results page, as shown in Figure 13.3. Click the **Pages** tab to view any matching pages.

If you're looking at all the results, it's not always easy to tell what's a Page and what's a group. Look for a link that says **Become a Fan** or **Become a Supporter** to indicate whether it's a Page or group. Another giveaway is to look at the total number of members. If it's a large number, chances are it's the organization's officially sanctioned Page.

When you find a Page you like, you can become a fan or supporter in just one click. Look for a **Become a Fan** or **Become a Supporter** link at the top of the Page. When you click the link, Facebook adds a small story about it on your profile page, saying something to the effect of "Sherry became a fan of Dr. Pepper." You friends can then see the story and comment, or follow the link to the Page and become a fan, too.

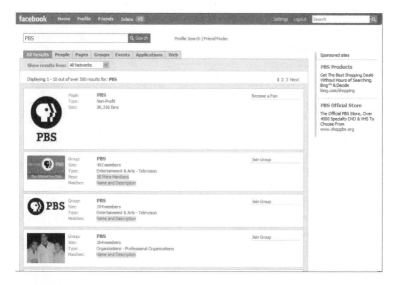

FIGURE 13.3   The results page displays any matches.

Once you're a fan, you're a subscribed member, so to speak. To view any updates of the Pages of which you're a fan, display the Home page and click the **Pages** link. This displays the news feeds from the Pages to which you're subscribed. You can also choose to view updates using your Inbox. Display your Inbox and click the **Updates** tab, as shown in Figure 13.4.

TIP

To unsubscribe from a Page, open the Page and look for a **Remove Me from Fans** link or something similar. You'll find it on the far-left side as you scroll down the Page. Just click the link, and you're no longer a fan.

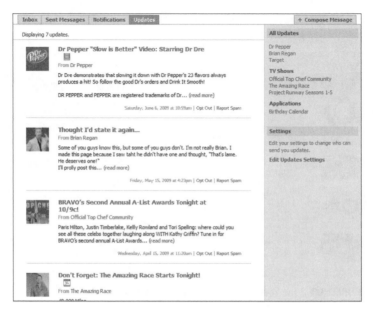

FIGURE 13.4   You can follow Page updates using your Inbox page and Updates tab.

Setting Up a Facebook Page

If you're the official representative of a business, organization, or public figure, you can set up a Page in Facebook. Before you get started, take time to gather all the elements you need and save yourself some effort. Here are a few things you'll need:

▶ A name for the Page. The name you choose cannot be changed later—it's permanent (unless the Page is deleted entirely).

▶ A photo to act as the Page's profile picture.

▶ Information about the company, organization, or public figure. Information may include contact information, address, background story, company history, and so on.

▶ Content, such as pictures for a photo gallery or video clips, or content generated by apps.

▶ A category, such as a local business, brand or product, or public figure. Within each of these main categories are subcategories for defining exactly what kind of organization you represent, such as a grocery store or travel agency, actor or comedian, and so on. The category you choose has everything to do with how the Page is indexed on Facebook. It might help to research other Pages to see how they are categorized before attempting to create your own Page.

> **CAUTION**
>
> If you're not authorized to create a Page and Facebook finds out, your account may be closed and the Page pulled from the site. Fan pages are not allowed unless created by an authorized person. If you'd rather create a fan page, you can do so with a group. See Lesson 10 to learn more.

Creating a New Page

After you've planned out what you need to display on the Page, you're ready to start building it. Follow these steps to create a new Page in Facebook:

1. Scroll to the bottom of any page and click the **Advertising** link.

Facebook opens the Facebook Advertising page.

2. Click the **Pages** link at the top.

Facebook displays the Facebook Pages information, as shown in Figure 13.5.

3. Click the **Create a Page** button in the upper-right corner.

The Create New Facebook Page form opens, as shown in Figure 13.6.

4. Click a category type. Try to choose a category that best matches the type of Page you're creating, such as a local business, a brand or product, or a public figure. Each of the three main categories will display a sub-category drop-down list you can use to be more specific.

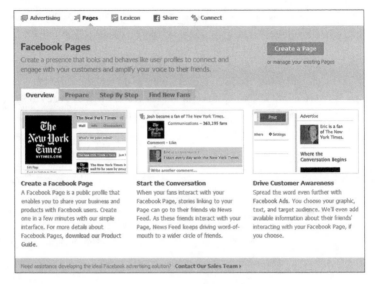

FIGURE 13.5   You can find your way to the Pages feature using the Advertising link.

5. Click the drop-down list to narrow down your selection even further.

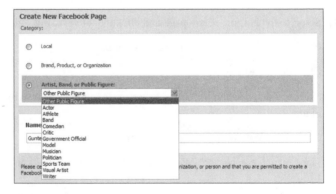

FIGURE 13.6   Narrow down your category as much as possible using the available options.

6. Type a name for the business, product, or public figure (see Figure 13.7).

FIGURE 13.7 Finish filling out the form and authorizing your approval to create the Page.

7. Click the authorization check box and type in your signature name.

8. Click **Create Page**.

A very blank Page opens, as shown in Figure 13.8. You can now begin filling in the content for the Page, as needed.

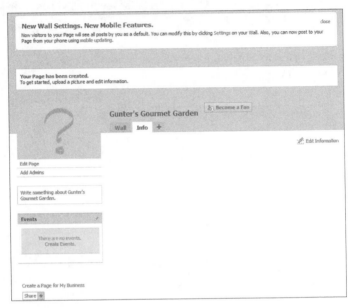

FIGURE 13.8 A blank Page opens, ready for you to add content, info, and a profile picture.

TIP

If it turns out you don't like any of the fields associated with the category you chose, you can delete the Page entirely and start all over again. To do so, click the **Edit Page** link under the profile picture area; then click the **Delete Page** link at the top of the next page. Facebook warns you about the deletion; click **Delete** to make it permanent. You can now start over and create a new Page using a more suitable category.

Filling Out Page Info

Filling out the Page's information is very similar to the way you filled out your profile page when you first created your Facebook account. You can edit various aspects of the Page, such as the Info tab, add a photo album, and so on. One of the first things you should do is add a photo or other image type (such as a logo or graphic) to serve as your Page's profile picture. To add a profile picture, click the picture area and then click the **Change Picture** link that appears. From the menu that pops up, you can upload a photo, take a new photo using your computer's camera, or choose an existing photo from an album. You upload a picture for a Page in the same way you uploaded a photo for your personal profile page. (See Lesson 2, "Setting Up a Profile," to learn more about uploading photos.)

As you look around the new Page, you'll see many of the same elements found on your own profile page, including tabs for various features (Wall, Info), a spot to add a blurb about the organization or person under the profile picture, and links for editing the Page or adding administrators. To add content to the Page to the Info tab, display the tab and click the **Edit Information** link, shown in Figure 13.9.

FIGURE 13.9 To edit the Info tab details, click the Edit Information link.

Depending on your Page's category, the information fields will vary. You can begin adding information to the Page (see Figure 13.10). When you finish, click the **Save Changes** button at the bottom of the Page. Click the **Done Editing** button to close out the fields entirely.

> TIP
>
> Don't forget to become a fan of your own Page! Click the **Become a Fan** or **Become a Supporter** link to subscribe like everyone else.

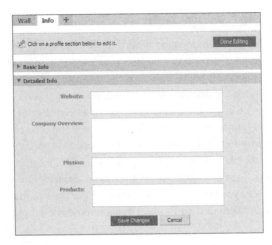

FIGURE 13.10   Your fields will vary based on which category of organization you chose when creating the Page.

You can edit your Page as much as you need. You can add photo albums, video clips, apps, and so on. When you're finally ready to publish the Page and make it public, click the **Publish This Page** link at the top of the screen, as shown in Figure 13.11. You don't have to publish the Page right away. You can skip this process and do it later.

FIGURE 13.11   Click the link in this box when you're finally ready to publish the Page.

> TIP
> You can take your Page "offline" for edits and publish it again when it's updated. Click the **Edit Page** link and click the **Edit** icon in the **Settings** options. You can then set the **Published Status** drop-down list to **Unpublished**.

Managing and Editing a Page

It's easy to manage a Page using your administrator powers. When the Page is published, you'll find links for editing the Page. Click the **Edit Page** link under the profile picture area to open the Page shown in Figure 13.12. From this Page, you can edit settings, Wall display, mobile settings, settings for various applications you're using with the Page, and more. The right side features links to various resources to help you with the Page, including links for adding new administrators to assist you with managing the content. You can also use this page to send out updates to your subscribers.

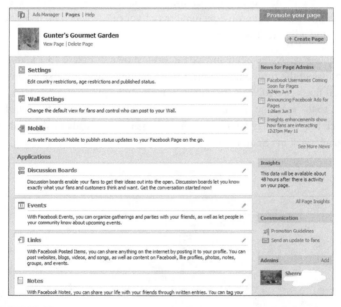

FIGURE 13.12   Open the Edit Page settings to make changes to various aspects of the Page.

To make changes to the settings, simply click an **Edit** button (look for the pencil icon) next to the area you want to edit and choose **Edit** from the pop-up menu. This displays fields or options for changing the associated settings. After your Page has been up and running for 48 hours, you can use the Insights feature to view data about demographics and activity of people accessing your Page.

To return to the Page after making changes, just click the **View Page** link at the top.

Sending Out Updates

You can alert your fans to new features, news, and other additions to your Page using Facebook's Updates feature (see Figure 13.13). This feature works much like a message you email that ends up in the recipient's Inbox. Unlike email messages, however, Page updates appear on a special tab page in the Inbox, called, appropriately, Updates. You can even target your update to subsets of your fans, such as subscribers from a certain area of the globe. To send out an update, look for the **Send an Update to Fans** link below the profile picture area of your Page and click it. You can also find a link to this on the Edit Page screen.

Facebook opens the Send an Update form, shown in Figure 13.13. You can fill out the form with a subject title and a message, just like a regular email message. You can also attach a photo, video, link, or other extra item to the message. To target the audience, click the **Target This Update** check box to display targeting options. When you're ready to send out the update, click the **Send** button.

FIGURE 13.13   Use the Send an Update page to send out a message to all of your fans.

Advertising Your Page

You can use your advertising dollars to promote your Page on Facebook. Facebook offers two kinds of advertising: pay by clicks or pay by views (also called *per impression* ads). With pay by clicks, you pay a set amount every time a user clicks your ad. With pay by views, you establish a price for 1,000 views of your ad. When creating an ad for Facebook, you can specify a target audience to help your ad reach the people you want. You can also specify a maximum amount to spend on the ad. You can learn all about advertising on Facebook by clicking the Advertising link at the bottom of any Facebook page. The Facebook Advertising page, shown in Figure 13.14, offers a step-by-step guide for planning and implementing an ad. You'll also find help with advertising regulations and rules on the site.

FIGURE 13.14   Facebook's Advertising feature offers step-by-step help with placing a promotional ad on the site.

Summary

In this lesson, you learned how to use Pages on Facebook. You learned how to find Pages, subscribe to Pages, and check their updates. You also saw how to make a new Page for your company or organization and then manage the Page after it's published. In the next lesson, you'll learn how to buy and sell stuff at the Facebook Marketplace.

The Facebook Marketplace

In this lesson, you learn how to sell, trade, and give stuff away locally on Facebook. You'll learn how to use the Marketplace app to browse items for sale and create your own listing.

What Is the Facebook Marketplace?

The Facebook Marketplace is a mutual effort from Facebook and Oodle, a network for classified ads online. Hoping to capture the growing Facebook user base, Facebook's Marketplace combines the social and interactive elements of its site with the growing popularity of online classifieds. Marketplace is another of Facebook's default applications available to all users. You can sell stuff in the Marketplace, buy stuff others are selling, or just give it away. You can search for specific items, sell items for a charity, or just see what everyone else is buying and selling online. You can sell household items, vehicles, and even houses in the Marketplace. You can also advertise for roommates, search for jobs, or look for an apartment to rent. The service is free, and best of all, you can conceivably know who you're buying from or selling to by checking out their profile pages when applicable. Although the Marketplace app is integrated into Facebook, it's managed by Oodle. The Marketplace feature has been available for awhile now, but it's just now beginning to pick up steam, particularly after the success of Craigslist and the advent of new site upgrades to Facebook in the spring of 2009.

Like other online classified ad sites, you can create listings for items you want to sell or give away. Your listings can include a photo of the item, details about it, and why you're selling it or giving it away. Others can come along and view your listing, ask questions, add comments, and make a deal. Because of Facebook's viral nature, someone can come along and comment about a listing, such as "I have one of these and I love it," or "I want to give away my couch to charity, too," and spread the word quickly throughout their networks of friends. The sale or donation of an item can generate other interests, conversations, and so on. You may be surprised at the outcome, such as finding out that someone shares the same hobby or cause as you.

The Marketplace offers four distinct categories for listings, as follows:

Items for Sale This category is for items you want to sell, such as household items, furniture, baby clothes, books, and so on.

Housing Use this category to look for houses and condos for sale, apartments to rent, roommates, and short-term housing situations.

Vehicles This category is for listing cars, motorcycles, campers, vehicle parts, boats, and other motorized vehicles.

Jobs This category lists jobs and job-wanted situations.

You peruse each category to see what's out there, for sale, for free, or for a charitable donation. Each category features subcategories.

CAUTION

Anytime you enter into the realm of buying and selling on the Internet, fraud and scam artists lurk around, ready to thwart your efforts. Be cautious, especially about deals that are too good to be true. Scammers offer all kinds of transactions that ultimately are illegal or rob you of your money, such as bounced checks, scams to send money to another country, or scams to steal your personal information. If your gut tells you something's wrong, it probably is. You can always report your suspicions; look for a **Report This Listing** link at the bottom of any ad. You can also alert Facebook when you encounter spam ads.

Navigating Around the Marketplace

To help you get a better idea of what you can do with the Marketplace, take a few moments to look around the pages. Figure 14.1 shows the Marketplace Home page, the "doorway," so to speak, to the online classified ads. You can access this page by clicking the **Marketplace** icon on the Applications bar, or by clicking the **Applications** button and then clicking **Marketplace**.

> NOTE
>
> If you're a new Facebook user, you may not see the Marketplace app listed among your applications. If this is the case, you can conduct a search for it and authorize its use. Simply type the keyword **Marketplace** in the Search box on the navigation bar; then press **Enter** or **Return**. From the Marketplace page, click the **Go to Application** button.

FIGURE 14.1   Facebook's Marketplace gateway.

As you can see in Figure 14.1, there are four main categories in the Marketplace: Items for Sale, Housing, Vehicles, and Jobs. Each of these categories has subcategories. You can expand or collapse the subcategories by clicking on the **More** link at the bottom of the main category. The bottom area below the categories displays the latest listings posted in your area.

Across the top of the Marketplace Home page are links for returning to the Home page, checking out charitable causes, and viewing your own listings. Just to the right is a **Search** box where you can conduct a search for an item or listing.

Most importantly, you'll notice a **Settings** link at the top, next to the Location label. You can click this link and specify a local area where you want to shop. To set your Marketplace location, follow these steps:

1. Click the **Settings** link to display the Location Settings dialog box shown in Figure 14.2.

FIGURE 14.2   You can specify a Marketplace location.

2. Click the **Search** drop-down menu and choose a country.

3. Click the **within** drop-down menu and choose a mileage option.

4. Type in a location, preferably a city near you.

5. Click **Submit**.

Facebook changes the Marketplace page to reflect the new location setting. You can now peruse listings in your area.

> **TIP**
>
> You can also subscribe to the Marketplace Page, the official application profile page about the app. By becoming a "fan," you can receive the latest updates about the app, and you can also participate on the Page's discussion boards. For example, you can find help from other users regarding a listing or transaction. To access the Page, type the keyword **Marketplace** in the Search box on the navigation bar and press **Enter** or **Return**. From the Marketplace page, click the **Become a Fan** link. See Lesson 13, "The Professional Side of Facebook: Pages," to learn more about Pages.

Looking at Listings

You can search for a specific item in the Marketplace, or you can browse the listings to see what people are selling in your area. For example, to look for items being offered for sale, look among the Items For Sale category. To browse, just click a subcategory under any main category area. Facebook then opens a results page, similar to Figure 14.3. Computer items are listed in this example.

As you peruse the listings, you can click a listing title to open its page. The listing page opens, looking very similar to a profile page, as shown in Figure 14.4. It includes the seller's profile picture, details about the item they're selling, a place for a photo of the item, recent listings, and an area at the bottom of the listing to ask a question or leave a comment. If you're interested in the item, click the **Contact** button at the top of the page and send the seller a message. You can also write on the listing's Wall, labeled Comments and Shouts, to ask a question.

You can click the **Share** button to open the Share dialog box and post a link to the ad on your profile page, or send a link to a friend to check out.

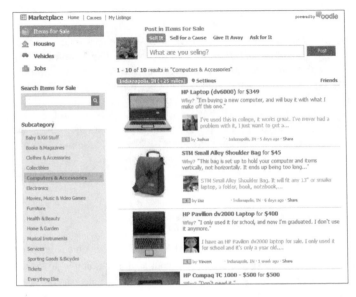

FIGURE 14.3   You can leisurely browse through the various subcategories to see what's listed in your area.

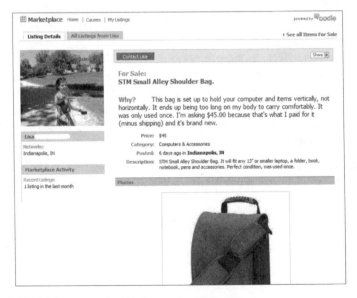

FIGURE 14.4   A typical ad listing on the Marketplace.

To search for a specific item, click in the **Search** box on the Marketplace page or on the listings page and type in the keyword or words you want to look up. Press **Enter** or **Return**, and Facebook displays any matching results. Facebook keeps track of your typed searches and lists them on the results page in case you want to use them again at a later time; just click the text to conduct a search.

CAUTION

Don't confuse the Marketplace Search box with the Search field on the Facebook navigation bar. They are used for two different types of searches: searching the Facebook site and searching the Marketplace.

When users create a new listing, they can choose from four types of ads, as follows:

> **Sell It**   These are items for sale.
>
> **Sell for a Cause**   These items are for sale, but the profits from the sale go to a designated charity.
>
> **Give It Away**   These are items people want to get rid of or trade for free.
>
> **Ask For It**   These are items people are specifically looking for and cannot seem to find elsewhere in the Marketplace.

When you're looking at Marketplace listings, you can filter the listings you browse by the four different types of ads. To do so, scroll down the listings page for the category you selected until you see the Types area, shown in Figure 14.5. Click the type to change the listings display.

If you click the **Causes** link at the top of the Marketplace page, you can view a page of charitable sites.

Click a charity from the list to view associated listings. These are typically items for sale with the proceeds going toward that particular charity. This is helpful when you want to support a particular charity.

FIGURE 14.5 You can filter the list to view items for sale, charity listings, items to give away, or items others are looking for.

Adding Your Own Listing

You can easily create your own ads in the Marketplace. To start a listing, click the **Post** link at the top of the appropriate category on the Marketplace Home page. This opens the listings page for the category.

Next, click an ad type: **Sell It**, **Sell for a Cause**, **Give It Away**, or **Ask For It**. After making your selection, click in the text box below and type a title for your ad; then click the **Post** button. It seems a little daunting at first, as if you're immediately creating an ad, much like you create a status update on your profile page. Don't worry—clicking the Post button does not create an instant ad. Instead, a dialog box opens where you can fill out more details about the listing. For example, if you're selling an item, the Sell It - Details box opens, as shown in Figure 14.6.

Depending on the type of listing you're creating, the form's fields will vary. You can fill out the form to create your ad. For example, you can redo the title (if needed), set a specific price for the item, tell why you're selling the item, choose a category for the item, add a description, and upload a picture. The fields marked with red asterisks are required—you cannot post the listing without filling them out.

FIGURE 14.6 You must fill out the ad's details before posting it in the Marketplace.

Although it's not required, adding a picture to your listing is always a good idea. It helps people know exactly what you're selling. You've already learned how to upload photos back in Lesson 8, "Sharing Photos," and the same technique is used to upload a photo for an ad.

After you've filled out everything, you can click **Submit** to post the ad. If you need to make any changes to the ad, open the My Listings page (click the **My Listings** link at the top of the Marketplace Home page), and click the **Edit** button next to the ad.

After you post an ad, it's up to you to monitor it, answer any questions that arise, and figure out how a buyer pays you when you reach an agreed-upon price. Because the Marketplace is designed to be local in nature, you can expect buyers to pick up the item at an arranged time and place, and pay with cash. Facebook's Marketplace does not offer a money service, like eBay's PayPal, so you're really left to your own devices.

To end a listing, after it's sold or when you give up on selling it, you can revisit the My Listings page and click the **Close** link.

Summary

In this lesson, you learned how to use Facebook's Marketplace to buy and sell items. You learned how to browse for items, search for specific items, and view items for sale, and about the four different types of listings. You also learned how to create and post your own listing. In the next lesson, you'll learn how to take Facebook on the road with you using the mobile features.

LESSON 15

Making Facebook Mobile

In this lesson, you learn how Facebook's mobile features work. You'll learn how to activate the texting feature to send and receive Facebook information and how to browse Facebook's mobile website using the special URL. Plus, you'll find out how easy it is to upload photos or videos from your cell phone's camera.

Facebook's Mobile Features Overview

If you simply cannot get enough of Facebook on your computer, you'll be happy to know you can access it through your mobile device and have Facebook at your fingertips wherever you go. You can use Facebook's mobile features to send and receive status updates, messages, Wall posts, and even send poke actions on your cell phone. You can tell Facebook to send you specific users' status updates, as well as what time frame messages are sent to your phone. Sounds like fun, right?

Text messaging is pretty standard mobile technology these days, and if your mobile device supports such features, chances are good that you can use it with Facebook's mobile capabilities. All text messages use a standardized mobile text transfer method, called SMS, short for *Short Message Service*, or MMS, short for *Multimedia Messaging Service*. If your mobile device supports SMS, you can send and receive text messages from Facebook. Depending on your service, you may be limited to the number and size of the messages (up to 140 characters). If your device supports MMS, you can go a step further and upload photos from your cell phone, for example, and post them onto your Facebook profile page.

If your mobile device features web browsing capabilities, you can visit
Facebook directly—in miniature form, of course—using the
m.facebook.com URL. You can do just about everything on the small-
scale page as you can on your full-blown web browser page. You can view
and change your status, check your friend's status, track events, view the
news feed stories, view photos, and see what's happening in your favorite
Facebook groups. You cannot visit Facebook's website without web
browsing capabilities, however, even if your cell phone just has text messaging features.

> NOTE
>
> If your mobile device happens to be one of the special smartphones
> out now, you can add a special mobile app for Facebook usage
> that's made especially for the phone. Look on the Facebook Mobile
> page for more information; click the **Mobile** link at the bottom of any
> Facebook page to learn more.

Activating Facebook Mobile for Text Messages

You can use your cell phone's text messaging features to send and receive
text to your Facebook account. For example, you can update your status,
post a comment on someone's Wall, or send someone a message. Before
you can start taking Facebook on the road with you, though, you first
have to activate the feature to work with your mobile device. Follow these
steps:

1. Click the **Mobile** link at the bottom of any Facebook page to
    open the Facebook Mobile page shown in Figure 15.1. You can
    read more about the various mobile features, if needed.

2. Click the **Edit Mobile Account** link on the far-right side of the
    page. (You can also click the **Settings** link on the navigation bar
    and then click the **Mobile** tab.)

    The My Account page opens, as shown in Figure 15.2.

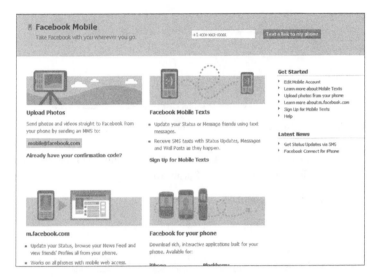

FIGURE 15.1 The Facebook Mobile page tells you all about the features you can use with a mobile device.

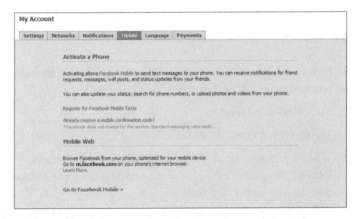

FIGURE 15.2 You can manage your mobile features using this tab on the My Account page.

3. Click the **Register for Facebook Mobile Texts** link.

The first of three boxes appears to help you set up your cell phone or other mobile device. Figure 15.3 shows the Activate Facebook Texts step 1 box.

FIGURE 15.3 Facebook displays the first of three steps.

4. Use the drop-down menus to select your country and mobile service provider (such as AT&T or Sprint, for example).

5. Click **Next** to continue.

The step 2 box opens, as shown in Figure 15.4.

FIGURE 15.4 Use step 2 to send for a confirmation code.

6. Follow the instructions displayed in the box, using your phone to send a text message to Facebook.

7. Click **Next** to continue.

The step 3 box opens, as shown in Figure 15.5.

8. When you receive the confirmation code back from Facebook (check your mobile device; the process could take several minutes), type the code in the field shown.

If you do not receive a confirmation code in a reasonable amount of time, resend the message again.

9. Click **Confirm**.

Facebook opens the Mobile app to the text settings page, shown in Figure 15.6, and displays a confirmation message at the top.

10. Select or deselect the text items you want to be sent to your mobile device.

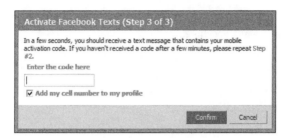

FIGURE 15.5 Use step 3 to enter your confirmation code.

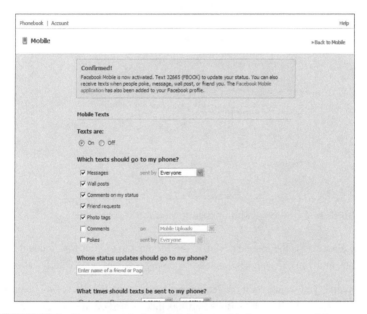

FIGURE 15.6 You can control what data is sent between your mobile device and Facebook using the settings on this page.

11. Scroll down the page (see Figure 15.7) and continue choosing which options you want to turn on or off, or specify:

You can specify which friends you want to receive updates from.

You can set a time limit for messages received from Facebook.

You can set a limit as to how many messages are sent, which is helpful if your cell phone account can only handle so many text messages.

You can also tell Facebook not to send you SMS messages while
you're using Facebook.

12. Click the **Save Preferences** button.

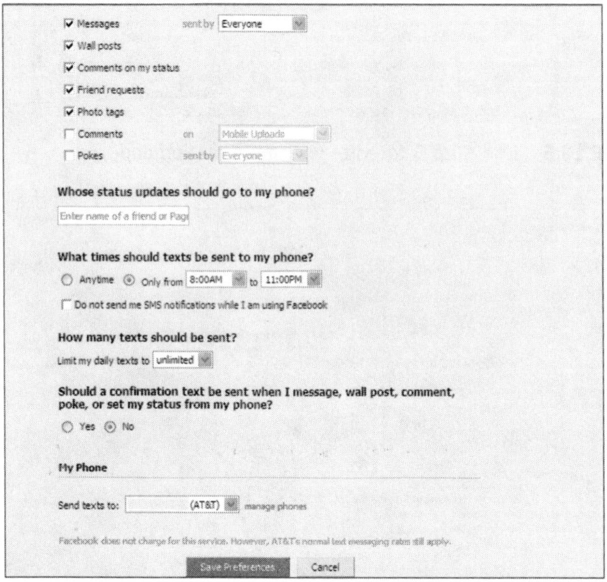

FIGURE 15.7   Scroll down the page to view more options.

Facebook adds the mobile device to the Mobile tab of your My Account
page, and you can start sending and receiving text messages with Facebook.

Anytime you want to edit the settings again, open the Facebook Mobile page
and click the **Edit Mobile Texts Settings** link located on the far-right side of
the page. You can also access the settings through your My Account page.

TIP

If you switch cell phone carriers later, you can revisit the Mobile tab
on your My Account page and remove the old phone and add the new
one using these same steps.

Sending Text Messages from a Mobile Device

Now that you've activated your Mobile account, you can start sending and receiving Facebook data. How does that work exactly? You can send messages using the codes listed in Table 15.1. The codes and text you send are directed to the 32665 number, which happens to spell FBOOK if you prefer keyboard letters instead of numbers. When directing your text to a specific Facebook user, be sure to use the person's full name. If there are other members with the same name, Facebook will ask you to confirm from a list of candidates it messages back to you. Simply make the correct choice, and on goes the message to the proper recipient.

TABLE 15.1   Facebook Texting Codes

Action	Code	Sample
Update your status	@	@ is visiting a museum!
Write on someone's Wall	wall	wall bob smith congrats on the promotion.
Send a message	msg	msg gail jones Hi, how r u?
Search for profile info	srch or search	srch bob smith or search bob smith
Get a cell number	cell	cell bob smith
Poke someone	poke	poke gail jones
Send a friend request	add	add bill miller
Write a note	note	note I'm having a great time in Florida.
Find help with texting	help	help

Surfing Facebook with a Mobile Browser

If your cell phone or mobile device features web browsing capabilities, you can access the mobile Facebook website, **m.facebook.com**. Use your mobile device's web browser to navigate to the URL; then log on using your account name and password. After you log on, you can bookmark the site to easily find it again.

You can also send your phone the text link to the site. To do so, open the Facebook Mobile page and click the **Text a link to my phone** link. This opens the dialog box shown in Figure 15.8. Check to make sure the correct cell number is displayed; then click the **Text link to my phone** button.

A link to m.facebook.com has been texted to the mobile phone 17656171361

Okay

FIGURE 15.8   Facebook lets you know the task was completed with this box.

Uploading Photos or Videos

You can upload photos or videos you take with your cell phone and add them to your Facebook profile page. You can do this only if your cell phone supports MMS (Multimedia Message Service) protocols. All you have to do is upload the photo or video to **mobile@facebook.com**.

If the phone you're using hasn't already been confirmed yet with Facebook's site, they'll send you back a confirmation code the first time you try an upload task. You'll have to log onto Facebook and enter the code on the **My Account** page in the **Mobile** tab (see Figure 15.2). After you've confirmed the phone, you can use it to upload more photos or videos to your profile page.

If you haven't used the Video app yet, be sure to add it to your account first by adding the tab to your profile page. See Lesson 9, "Sharing Videos," to learn more. To learn more about uploading and editing photo albums, see Lesson 8, "Sharing Photos."

You can also upload notes using a similar method; send the upload to **notes@facebook.com**.

Summary

In this lesson, you learned how to use Facebook's mobile features. You learned how to activate your Facebook Mobile account and send status updates from your cell phone. You also learned how to text messages and other Facebook actions to your friends. You found out how to access Facebook using a web browser on a mobile device, and how to upload photos and videos to your profile page.

Now that you've completed the final lesson, you're ready to venture out on your own and explore Facebook with confidence. Good luck and happy networking, socially speaking that is. I'll see you online!

Index

How can we make this index more useful? Email us at indexes@samspublishing.com

FREE Online Edition

Your purchase of **Sams Teach Yourself Facebook in 10 Minutes** includes access to a free online edition for 45 days through the Safari Books Online subscription service. Nearly every Sams book is available online through Safari Books Online, along with more than 5,000 other technical books and videos from publishers such as Addison-Wesley Professional, Cisco Press, Exam Cram, IBM Press, O'Reilly, Prentice Hall, and Que.

SAFARI BOOKS ONLINE allows you to search for a specific answer, cut and paste code, download chapters, and stay current with emerging technologies.

Activate your FREE Online Edition at www.informit.com/safarifree

> **STEP 1:** Enter the coupon code: DKIEGDB.

> **STEP 2:** New Safari users, complete the brief registration form. Safari subscribers, just log in.

If you have difficulty registering on Safari or accessing the online edition, please e-mail customer-service@safaribooksonline.com